Consciousness and Near Death Experiences

Consciousness and Near Death Experiences

Gerhard D. Wassermann DSc, FIBiol, FIMA, FIEE
Former Reader in the Theory and Philosophy of Biology
University of Newcastle upon Tyne

Copyright © Year I (2001)
by Gerhard D Wassermann and Mandrake of Oxford
First English Edition

All rights reserved. No part of this work may be reproduced or utilized in any form by any means electronic or mechanical, including *xerography, photocopying, microfilm*, and *recording*, or by any information storage system without permission in writing from the author.

Published by
Mandrake of Oxford
PO Box 250
OXFORD
OX1 1AP (UK)

A CIP catalogue record for this book is available from the British Library and the US Library of Congress.

ISBN 1 869928 628

Printed & bound by Antony Rowe Ltd, Eastbourne

Autobiographical Note About The Author

Professor Gerhard D. Wassermann is a Biologist and Philosopher. He graduated from Queen Mary College, University of London with first class Honours in Mathematics, and then obtained a Ph.D. in Quantum Mechanics from the University of London. After working for a while in Theoretical Acoustics (horn design) with Tannoy Products, Acoustical Engineers, he was invited by (the later) Nobel Laureate Sir Neville Mott to join his department at Bristol as Research Assistant to Prof. Herbert Fröhlich FRS.

Before this the author had for an extended period studied Biology at Birkbeck College, University of London. At Bristol the author also colaborated with (later) Professor Emil Wolf (now USA). After Bristol the author joined the University of Newcastle upon Tyne as a Lecturer. Later he became a Reader in the Theory and Philosophy of Biology in the same university. He also became an associate editor of the *Bulletin of Mathematical Biology*. Subsequently he became a visiting professor at the Hebrew University of Jerusalem (1980) (the invitation came from Prof. Fanny Doljanski of the Hebrew University-Hadassah Medical School Jerusalem (The Hubert H. Humphrey Center for Experimental Medicine and Cancer Research)).

In 1984 he became a visiting professor at the Institute of Evolution of the University of Haifa (Israel). The invitation came from the Director, Professor Eviatar Nevo, who is a Foreign Member of the USA National Academy of Science and a Foreign Member of the Linnean Society (UK), whose foreign membership is restricted to 50, and Nevo is a world leader in evolutionary studies.

In his career the author did research in Quantum Mechanics, Theoretical Optics, Theoretical Developmental Biology, Theory of Evolution. Biophilosophy, Philosophy of Science and Philosophy of Mind. He has published many papers in prestigious journals (subject to peer review) and seven books. The author also lectured for many years in Quantum Mechanics and other branches of Theoretical Physics at undergraduate and postgraduate levels in the University of Newcastle upon Tyne.

He also gave numerous invited guest lectures in the UK and abroad. He has also been invited as a speaker at several important international conferences (e.g. at the 7th International Congress of Logic, Methodology and Philosophy of Science, at Salzburg in 1983). Again, in August 1984 he attended the International Conference on Systems Research, Informatics and Cybernetics as a speaker at Baden Baden (Germany).

Note. The author's highly mechanistic theoretical work in Developmental Biology and other branches of Theoretical Biology could only get into its stride about 1965–1972 after modern molecular biology had emerged sufficiently. Much of the author's theorizing in these fields is based on molecular biology. The author also developed a major theory of paranormal phenomena which was published by Mandrake of Oxford in a book titled *Shadow Matter And Psychic Phenomena*.

The author is also a Fellow of the Institute of Mathematics and its Applications and was recently (1989) elected a Fellow of the Institute of Biology. He has also been awarded a DSc from the University of London (31.3.2000) and is a chartered Biologist.

Contents

Autobiographical Note About The Author 5
Preface 9

1 Fenwick's Versus Blackmore's And Jansen's Views On The General Nature Of Near Death Experiences (NDEs). 15
1.1 Introduction 15
1.2 Blackmore's and Fenwick's Views 17
1.3 NDEs and Anoxia 19
1.4 NDEs and Hypercarbia 20
1.5 The supposed Role of Endorphins in NDEs 21
1.6 OBEs and NDEs 22
1.7 Critique of Blackmore's Theory of OBEs 26
1.8 The 'Afterlife Hypothesis' and Mechanistic Materialism 29
1.9 Reality and the Shadow Matter Brain 31
1.10 Blackmore's Arguments against the Afterlife Hypothesis 33
1.11 The Directivity (or Purpose) of Life 38
1.12 Jansen's Approach to the NDE 41
1.13 Testability of the Shadow Matter Theory of paranormal Phenomena 48

2 Localized versus non-localized consciousness and mentality 51
2.1 The Heritage of Monotheism 51
2.2 C.J.S. Clarke's Vista of Non-Locality 52
2.3 Mind as a generic Term and some Remarks on Epiphenomenalism . 54
2.4 The Case for localized mentality (including Consciousness.) 56
2.5 Localization of Mentality versus Non-localization in Physics 58
2.6 The Shadow Matter Brain as a Property-Detector System 61
2.7 Localization within the Soul (= Shadow Matter brain) 65
2.8 Genetic Determination of Localization within the Soul 70
2.9 The Nonlocality of secondary encoded Mentality 72
2.10 Aspects of Personal Identity 73

3. Possible Mechanisms Of The Near Death Experience (NDE) 81
- 3.1 The possible Machinery of Out-of-the-Body Experiences (OBEs) ... 81
- 3.2 Explaining the Tunnel Experience (TE) 83
- 3.3 Back to Moody's idealized Account of a NDE 89
- 3.4 Further Explanation of the Machinery of the Life-Review 98
- 3.5 Some Views on the Nature of Powerful Scientific Theories 108

4 The Conjectured Nature Of Survival 113
- 4.1 The likely Immortality of the Soul 113
- 4.2 Personal Identity during Life and Death 115
- 4.3 Indefinite Evolution of Surviving Souls 117
- 4.4 The Importance of Spontaneous Cases 118
- 4.5 The Targeting of specific other Souls 120
- 4.6 Locations of surviving Souls in Heaven and Hell A 'Dual Hereafter Theory' 121
- 4.7 Do Souls have a personal Choice? 124
- 4.8 The Problem of Evil 125
- 4.9 Mentality of surviving Souls and Extraterrestrial Souls 126
- 4.10 The Likely Evolution of Souls 127
- 4.11 Is there bodily Resurrection? 128
- 4.12 What about 'Life' in Heaven? 137
- 4.13 Creation of Souls 139
- 4.14 Properties of disembodied Souls 141

5 Reincarnation and Survival 143
- 5.1 Introductory Remarks on Reincarnation 143
- 5.2 Class Characteristics of Reincarnation Phenomena 146
- 5.3 Further Discussion of the likely Mechanisms of Reincarnation 149
- 5.4 A very few Case Histories of Reincarnations 152
- 5.5 Additional Comments on the Findings of Stevenson 158
- 5.6 Coda 159
- **Bibliography** 161
- **Author Index** 168
- **Subject Index** 171

Preface

It is widely believed that mechanistic materialism, as accepted by many scientists, as well as non-scientists, is incompatible with the possibility of survival of the human personality after bodily death. That this belief may be completely wrong was already shown in my previous book *Shadow Matter And Psychic Phenomena* (Wassermann, 1993, Mandrake, Oxford). While my arguments in the latter book left the likelihood of survival an open question, they suggested possible mechanisms of survival. But they did not go far enough.

In this book I shall argue that the available evidence suggests strongly that survival is highly probable or, if you like, nearly certain. To start with, in Chapter 1, I shall discuss Dr. Sue Blackmore's view that 'near death experiences' (NDEs) can be explained in terms of brain physiology. In view of Dr. Peter Fenwick's (1994) criticisms of Blackmore's proposed mechanisms, however, it seems obligatory to discard most of Blackmore's theory of NDEs. However her book, as a source of facts, concerning NDEs (and 'out of the body experiences' [OBEs] which are parts of NDEs in many cases), is very valuable.

Dr. Fenwick is not only Chairman of the Council of the Scientific and Medical Network but he is emeritus Consultant Clinical Neuropsychiatrist at the Maudsley Hospital and Consultant Clinical Neurophysiologist at the Radcliffe Infirmary and a Senior Lecturer at the Institute of Psychiatry (etc.).

In Chapter 3 I shall advance a new theory of NDEs, based on my Shadow Matter theory of paranormal phenomena, which will be presented in an improved version. I shall propose how one could explain in terms of my Shadow Matter model the various features of NDEs. These include (to cite Blackmore, 1993) paranormal knowledge (already explained in Wassermann, 1993), the tunnel, the golden light, the OBE state (already largely explained in Wassermann, 1993), the voice or presence, the appearance of deceased relatives, beautiful vistas etc. In particular, I shall augment the previously postulated machinery of psi-phenomena (e.g. of OBEs) and introduce some new machinery for NDEs. In this way I shall attempt to show that NDEs can be fully mechanistically and materialistically explained.

Thus, the present book, together with its predecessor (Wassermann, 1993), provides a powerful and comprehensive theory of paranormal phenomena, and several major explanations of this book (e.g. my theory of reincarnation phenomena) are novel and the theory is *scientific* in that it is mechanistic and materialistic. My explanations, however, differ totally from most of those given by Blackmore, and the mechanisms proposed are not based on neural mechanisms. The notion that Shadow Matter could play a central part not only in paranormal phenomena but also in NDEs is a continuation of my earlier views of Wassermann (1993). The notion of Shadow Matter used here is a variant of the notion of Shadow Matter put forward by Kolb *et al.* (1985) in the leading science journal *Nature* (London).

There are people who believe that mentality is *localized* in the Shadow Matter brain (e.g. the present writer), while others (e.g. C.J.S. Clarke (1995)) believe that mind is not localized. In Chapter 2, I shall discuss the issue of the localization of mind or otherwise. Those who advocate non-localization of mind are apt to disregard OBEs (e.g. Clarke, 1995) and their implications for the localization issue, and, hence, they also disregard NDEs which frequently include OBEs. Admittedly the issue of the localization of mind (or of consciousness which is one aspect of mentality) is metaphysical and, hence, not testable. Nevertheless the evidence from OBEs allows one to carry the metaphysical debate further than is customary in the absence of OBEs, leading to considerable *explanatory insights*.

Another metaphysical creed is epiphenomenalism, which can, I believe, neither be proved to be valid nor refuted. Numerous people who realized that epiphenomenalism forms a possible bastion of mechanistic materialism, thought that epiphenomenalism could be falsified (e.g. Popper and Eccles (1977) or Clarke (1995)). But closer inspection of their arguments indicates that the alleged refutations of epiphenomenalism are invariably invalid (cf. Wassermann (1979, 1994) and Chapter 2 below). Conversely, those who read the refutations try to find fault with them, and so the metaphysical battle continues indefinitely.

In my opinion the metaphysical nature of epiphenomenalism is not a new philosophical insight, but has long been realized by many philosophers, but apparently not by Popper and various other people. There is, of course, nothing to debar people (e.g. philosophers) from adopting certain metaphysical positions, provided they do not think that these positions are rigorously logically or scientifically defensible.

This applies also to the issue of survival of the human personality after bodily death. Although (see Chapter 4) there exist numerous indicators which may convince many people that genuine survival occurs, final proof may not be possible. Granted that even if the existing evidence may convince many people (e.g. the present author, who is a mechanistic materialist, and many spiritualists). Perhaps the strongest pointer towards survival comes, in my opinion, from reincarnation phenomena, which I shall discuss in Chapter 5 and which I did not discuss in terms of my Shadow Matter theory in my earlier book (Wassermann, 1993). But although reincarnation may, perhaps, via the mechanisms of my theory, help to convince people of survival, it offers no final proof. All we can get, at best, are indirect pointers that survival *could* exist.

However compelling these pointers may be, they do not prove survival to exist, although no arguments to the contrary do firmly rule out survival. I realize, of course, that many spiritualists have not carefully studied the metaphysics of this situation and are easily swept off their feet by evidence which remains insufficient to prove survival. One can certainly accept (as I do) survival as a metaphysical hypothesis without claiming that evidence like NDEs, reincarnation etc. prove the existence of survival. Survival remains a matter of metaphysical belief. I owe much to the writings of Professor Ian Stevenson, the Carlson Professor of Psychiatry at the University Health Science Centre, Charlottesville, Virginia USA, who is a world leader on reincarnation phenomena. We met in Newcastle some years ago.

I have tried to come to terms with the most difficult issue of all. If the bad as well as the good survive, then are the bad punished in a hereafter and the good rewarded? This may seem a highly naive question to scientists and to those versed in moral philosophy. Yet, the question how we could survive is perhaps far more important than the likelihood that we survive. I realize, of course, that a vast amount has been written by numerous philosophers and thinkers of all kinds on these topics, and that one is dealing here, once more, with metaphysical issues.

What happens to an arch-criminal and vast-scale mass murderer like Hitler in the hereafter, and are the Jews, who that brute murdered, to be rewarded and reinstated in a glorious afterlife? Are these possibilities just wishful thinking or, as I am apt to believe, are they parts of a reality? Although there exist, obviously warped and criminal minds, there also exist great and noble individuals. Perhaps life on Earth has evolved so as to produce human mentality (alas the bad with the good) which, after death, carries on and sometimes perpetuates the glory of our finest thinking.

Newcastle upon Tyne
August 1998
G.D.W.

Dedicated To Two Daring Men

Professor Ian Stevenson
Pioneer in the Study of Reincarnation Phenomena

and

In Memory of Raoul Wallenberg who saved the lives of an estimated 100,000 Hungarian Jews from the death camps by issuing them with false papers (Cited from the *Times* 23. 12. 1996, p.4)
Wallenberg was 'one of the greatest heroes of the Second World War' (Cited from *Radio Times* 24. 11. 1998 p. 110)

14 Gerhard D Wassermann

1 Fenwick's Versus Blackmore's And Jansen's Views On The General Nature Of Near Death Experiences (NDEs).

1.1 Introduction

In 1993 I published a novel kind of theory of psychic phenomena (Wassermann, 1993 sometimes-abbreviated W93). The theory was published in a book titled *Shadow Matter And Psychic Phenomena*. Although I devoted a whole chapter to the issue of possible survival of the human personality after bodily death, I did not go remotely far enough. This book aims to go much further and tries to suggest that, contrary to commonsense, it seems physically quite possible that an important component of each of us survives death. It is a part of this component which during life and death carries our memories and our ability to think, feel etc. There are, of course, plenty of people, who call themselves 'rationalists' and who ridicule those who believe in the survival of the human personality after bodily death.

After all, they claim, the human body, notably its brain, is the carrier of our memories and intellectual capacities. When we die the brain disintegrates (or is cremated), unless specifically preserved. So how can our mental faculties survive when their physical carriers disappear? This, however, as I shall argue in this book (see also W93), simply does not follow. The fact that simplistic arguments may convince unsophisticated people, is no evidence for the validity of these arguments.

If there is, indeed, survival, then what are the mechanisms of survival? These, if they exist, are likely to be linked to the machinery of death and dying. Perhaps a valuable guide to the possible machinery of death and dying might be obtained by attempts to elucidate the conceivable mechanisms of Near Death Experiences

(NDEs). These have been studied for many years by various people. One of the most renowned studies of this kind can be found in Moody's (1976) book *Life After Life* which is a pioneering work.

Much interesting material can also be found in Susan Blackmore's (1993) book *Dying To Live* even if one prefers different interpretations of NDEs. My own theorizing differs drastically from Blackmore's, which has been critically assessed by Dr. Peter Fenwick (1994). He is a former consultant clinical neuropsychiatrist at the Maudsley Hospital and Senior Lecturer at the Institute of Psychiatry and was (or still is) President of IANDS (International Association for Near Death Studies) UK.

A typical NDE has several characteristic components. Some of these are present in many other (but not necessarily all) NDEs. A classic summary of a somewhat extrapolated and generalized case history of a NDE was first given by Moody (1976, p. 21) in the following passage which was more recently repeated by Blackmore (1993, p.7). This passage seems to me to be so important, that no serious book on the subject should dispense with it. Moody wrote in his idealized account of a NDE:

'A man is dying and as he reaches the point of greatest physical distress, he hears himself pronounced dead by his doctor. He begins to hear an uncomfortable noise, a loud ringing or buzzing, and at the same time feels himself moving very rapidly through a long dark tunnel. After this, he suddenly finds himself outside of his own physical body, but still in the immediate physical environment, and he sees his own body from a distance, as though he is a spectator. He watches the resuscitation attempt from his unusual vantage-point and is in a state of emotional upheaval.'

'After a while, he collects himself and becomes accustomed to his odd condition. He notices that he still has a 'body', but one of a very different nature and with very different powers from the physical body he has left behind. Soon other things begin to happen. Others come to meet and to help him. He glimpses the spirits of relatives and friends who have already died, and a loving warm spirit of a kind he never encountered before—a being of light—appears before him. This being asks him a question, nonverbally, to make him evaluate his life and helps him along by showing him a panoramic, instantaneous playback of the major events of his life.

At some point he finds himself approaching some sort of barrier or border, apparently representing the limit between earthly life and the next life. Yet he finds that he must go back to earth, that the time for his death has not yet come. At this point he resists, for by now he is taken up with his experience in the afterlife and does not want to return. He is overwhelmed by intense feelings of joy, love and peace. Despite his attitude, though, he somehow reunites with his physical body and lives.'

'Later he tries to tell others, but he has trouble doing so. In the first place he can find no human words adequate to describe these unearthly episodes. He also finds that others scoff, so he stops telling other people. Still, the experience affects his life profoundly, especially his views about death and its relationship to life.'

As Moody stresses, this 'composite' case is extrapolated from many known cases and does not represent a single experienced case. Indeed, any one of the sub-components of the 'composite' case may be found in some of the cases studied but not in others. Hence the total case history may vary substantially between cases, although some case histories may be strikingly similar. How is one to explain these extraordinary phenomena and their *repeatable class characteristics?* There have been various attempts to provide suitable explanations, but almost all of these seem to be inadequate.

Accordingly, I shall devote part of this monograph to providing a new and comprehensive theory of near-death experiences (NDEs). This theory will in parts be based on my recent theory of psychic phenomena, which I published in (W93). Before I go ahead with this I shall first describe in essentials Fenwick's (1994) critique of Blackmore's (1993) theory of NDEs. Otherwise I could be accused of gross ignorance of Blackmore's interesting attempt to establish a suitable theory.

1.2 Blackmore's and Fenwick's Views

Fenwick (1994) starts by noting that Dr. Blackmore 'has written a wonderful book'. This, indeed, is likely to be the case as far as the mere description of the NDE phenomena is concerned, although there are other books, which are, perhaps, equally strong in this respect. However, when it comes to her theorizing about these phenomena, Fenwick's views of this theorizing are, on the whole, not encouraging at all. Blackmore rejects the 'after-life hypothesis' for interpreting NDEs but favours the 'dying-brain hypothesis' for explaining NDEs. She also points out (as does Fenwick (1994)) that one can have a NDE without being near death (Blackmore 1993, pp. 41 ff). Thus, on p. 41 (l.c.) she states that '*there is lots of evidence for NDE-type experiences in people who are not close to dying.*' At least this can be asserted for NDE components. Typically, 'out of the body experiences' (OBEs) which may appear as part of a NDE, can occur to people who are not in the process of dying.

One could argue that in a dying brain a battery of processes of kind X could lead to a NDE, whereas in a normal brain, in some circumstances, processes of kind Y could produce a NDE. While this kind of argument could be valid, it does not explain the precise nature and mechanisms of processes of kind X and processes of kind Y. It is for these reasons alone that I shall try to explain in terms of precise mechanisms the nature of NDEs.

At this stage let me interrupt and turn briefly to Fenwick's final critique of Blackmore's book. Fenwick (1994 p. 76) writes:

> 'What we call "near death" experiences, as Sue (Blackmore) is careful to point out right at the beginning of her book, can occur not only near death but at other times when brain function is not disturbed in any way. So, at best, the dying brain hypothesis can only provide a partial explanation. More significantly we have to deal with the question of brain function itself, and whether an objective third person description of neuronal function can ever be sufficient to give a first person perspective and explanation. Until we can answer this question, the near death experience must ultimately remain an enigma.'

Suppose, as is often acknowledged, and certainly by the present author, neuronal functions should (or partly can) be explained in terms of appropriate materialistic mechanisms based on suitably postulated brain machinery. Then subjective experiences can be interpreted as epiphenomena (= non-material byproducts) of the functioning of materialistic systems. Traditionally these systems are pronounced to be the ordinary brain matter itself. However, I have argued elsewhere (Wassermann, 1993) that, perhaps more plausibly, the material carrier and producer of conscious experiences could be the *Shadow Matter Brain* which, by hypothesis, is attached to the ordinary matter brain. But, even when viewed in this way, subjective experiences (but not their producing machinery) must remain an enigma.

According to Wassermann (1993) the (epiphenomenally) consciousness-producing systems are *material* systems, although not ordinary matter systems but Shadow Matter systems. Thus, although we cannot explain what conscious experiences are as entities, we can explain, perhaps with luck, the brain and Shadow Matter brain machinery that, by its functions, generates these experiences as epiphenomena. Conscious experiences *per se* may ultimately remain enigmas. This does not debar us from explaining which brain machinery and/or Shadow Matter brain machinery is accompanied by these conscious experiences. So near death experiences (which *are* conscious experiences) must remain enigmas.

This, however, does not rule out mechanistic suggestions of which type of machinery, and its working, NDEs could be byproducts. I conclude that although a *complete* explanation of the nature of NDEs cannot be given now, or perhaps ever, any more than the nature of consciousness can be fully explained, *partial* mechanistic explanations of NDEs may be possible. (A point disregarded by Fenwick (1994), who seems to believe that a partial explanation is not valid until a complete explanation has been obtained). In fact, some parts of this book will be devoted to such partial mechanistic explanations of NDEs.

The assumed feasibility of partial explanations of NDEs, however, does not mean that Blackmore's (1993) ingenious partial explanations of NDEs (in terms of the 'dying brain hypothesis') are necessarily the best and only available mechanistic partial explanations of NDEs. In fact, Fenwick's (1994) critical discussion of Blackmore's (1993) theory of NDEs casts doubt on this possibility. Let me, therefore, return to Fenwick's critique, where I departed earlier.

1.3 NDEs and Anoxia

To explain partially a typical NDE, some theorists have claimed that cerebral anoxia (no oxygen) could be the cause. There have been various arguments against the cerebral anoxia hypothesis. Fenwick (l.c. p. 74) notes that lowered brain oxygen levels of sufficient degree 'disorganizes mentation and leads to confusion and disorientation, with severe degradation of recent memory'. Yet, in a typical NDE there is notable clarity, and, as Fenwick also points out, a strong memory of the NDE is formed. *Prima facie* this speaks against the anoxia hypothesis of NDEs. Perhaps against this one could cite Blackmore's (1993, p. 55) argument. She states that:

> 'The speed of oxygen loss may be most relevant. Very fast onset of anoxia is rather like alcoholic intoxication and can also lead to sudden black-out with no experience. On the other hand very slow anoxia produces confusion and lassitude quite unlike NDEs. This leads to the possibility that NDEs come about with intermediate speeds of oxygen decline. Drowning is one example and is a common trigger for NDEs. With the heart still working and some oxygen still available in the circulating blood, the anoxia will not be as fast as with sudden cardiac arrest.'

It is not obvious why Fenwick in the review of Blackmore's book, cited above, does not cite and discuss Blackmore's argument, just quoted, concerning the possibility that medium fast anoxia could be the trigger of NDEs. The presumptive reason why Fenwick (1994) seems to disregard Blackmore's argument relating to the speed of oxygen loss can probably be found in Fenwick's (1994) argument (l.c. p.74). He states that 'there is abundant clinical evidence that hypoxia *of any degree* (italics mine) disorganizes mentation and leads to confusion and disorientation, with severe degradation of recent memory.' Thus, hypoxia, irrespective of its speed of onset, whether mild or severe, leads to symptoms that are at variance with those of NDEs. I believe that Fenwick's argument lays the ghost of the anoxia thesis, as presented by Blackmore and others.

1.4 NDEs and Hypercarbia

The hypothesis of NDE triggering by medium speed of anoxia onset is apparently not only invalid but provides only one suggested physical cause of NDEs. An alternative hypothetical cause is sometimes attributed to hypercarbia (Blackmore, 1993), i.e. an excess of brain carbon dioxide, as the origin of NDEs. As Blackmore (1993) notes, indeed excess levels of inspired carbon dioxide can mimic many aspects of a typical NDE (Meduna, 1950). Fenwick (1994), however, asks whether the degree of induced hypercarbia that leads to these mimicked effects 'would not also be accompanied by a degree of anoxia sufficient to produce confusion and disorientation' in contrast to a NDE. In addition Fenwick (1994, p. 75) notes that 'Meduna also mentions that a number of patients [treated with carbon dioxide] had myoclonic jerks and motor movements, and some even got up and acted out their experiences. This does not happen in NDEs.'

The fact that apparently *not all* of Meduna's patients, but only 'a number' of them had myoclonic jerks etc. does not rule out that some of those patients who did not have myoclonic jerks (etc.) could not have had genuine NDEs.

We have seen that Blackmore considers the possibility that anoxia could explain the main features of the NDE such as the tunnel and light phenomena (which I mentioned briefly in the passage quoted from Moody above). Thus, Moody states that the NDE percipient (at the appropriate stage of some NDEs) 'feels himself [or herself] moving very rapidly through a long dark tunnel.' There are also many NDE percipients' encounters with the 'being of light' (see p. 3).

In a somewhat different context, Blackmore (1993, p. 50) notes that 'NDEs can occur in people who obviously do not have anoxia.' In such cases Blackmore will have to deal with Fenwick's appropriate comment 'that both tunnel and light phenomena can occur in the absence of anoxia.' Perhaps Blackmore might be tempted to argue that tunnel and light phenomena are produced, when anoxia is not present by mechanisms of type A, but when anoxia is present they are produced by a completely, or partially, different set of mechanisms of type B. While this is not impossible it seems to me unlikely. My reasons for saying so are that I have produced a theory, given later in this book, which, apparently, can explain many aspects of NDE experiences in the presence or absence of anoxia in similar terms. While one cannot rule out dogmatically that anoxia could be, in some NDEs, an initial trigger, it does not seem to be a likely instrument for bringing about the details of NDEs.

1.5 The supposed Role of Endorphins in NDEs

Let me now turn to another serious criticism by Fenwick of Blackmore's theory. Fenwick writes that Blackmore:

'suggests that the feelings of joy and bliss which are the central point of the NDE are due to the release by anoxia of endorphins, opiate-like chemicals known to produce feelings of tranquility. The hypothesis is complicated as it also suggests that areas in the temporal lobe which may possibly mediate emotions are also involved due to abnormal electrical discharges (a sort of epilepsy). These two factors she suggests lead to the mystical experiences of the NDE. The problem with this explanation is that there are many accounts of wide mystical states in every way identical to that of the NDE which occur in a normally functioning brain. Thus the endorphin theory must fail.'

In the preceding quote it is, perhaps, a little surprising that Fenwick does not simply dismiss Blackmore's endorphin hypothesis from the start. She suggests that the endorphins involved in the NDE are released by anoxia. But Fenwick has already noted that anoxia does not produce the central effects of the NDE. In fact, as noted above, Blackmore (1993) states herself that 'NDEs can occur in people who obviously do not have anoxia.' Perhaps Fenwick, rightly, wanted to show that apparently other basic features of the endorphin hypothesis of NDEs are either invalid or, at least, seriously questionable.

Fenwick is also convincing when he states that Blackmore's epilepsy involvement thesis

'to those of us who deal in epilepsy [like Fenwick], is so atypical of any epileptic process, that it too must be ruled out of court. Every day in hospital endorphin agonists are given by the bucketful to control pain, but no mystical states result.'

1.6 OBEs and NDEs

Now let me turn to another aspect of the NDE. One of the principal components of many, or most, NDEs is the '*out of the body experience*' (OBE), which can also occur independently of a NDE, in apparently perfectly normal people. To give readers unfamiliar some idea of what a typical OBE can be like let me cite some examples. Here is a case history from Broughton (1991, p. 244). He relates 'the experience of a British woman who was hospitalized and operated on for peritonitis. She subsequently became very ill with pneumonia and was confined to bed. The ward was L-shaped and from her bed she could not see around the corner.'

'One morning I felt myself *floating upwards* [italics are mine] and found I was looking down on the rest of the patients. *I could see myself* propped up against pillows, very white and ill. I saw the sister and nurse rush to my bed with oxygen. Then everything went blank. The next I remember was opening my eyes to see the sister bending over me. I told her what had happened: but at first she thought I was rambling. Then I said, 'There is a big woman sitting up in bed with her head wrapped in bandages; and she is knitting something with blue wool. She has a very red face. This certainly shook her; as apparently the lady concerned had a mastoid operation and was just as I described...'

'She was not allowed out of bed; and of course I hadn't been up at all. After several other details, such as the time by the clock on the wall (which had broken down) I convinced her that at least something strange had happened to me.'

Here we can discern several *class characteristics* typical of many OBEs (but not present in all OBEs). In the case just cited, the OBEr *sees his or her own body from the outside.* Again, there is a *perceived upward floating.* Also the percipient can clearly perceive objects, three dimensionally and normally coloured, in her surroundings *as could be seen from the position which the percipient claims to have taken up by floating in space.*[1]

The experienced upward movement (or upward floating) in many OBEs is also quoted, incidentally, in another case history by Celia Green (1976, p. 116), The fascinating account is too long to be given in full, so I shall only cite the relevant part. The percipient was walking with, and talking to, a friend and reported that

'suddenly I seemed to be 50–100 ft. above my body. I could see us both walking along in the shallow bowl of hills, and could see small gestures. I seemed to be floating above myself rather like a balloon attached to a string, but I could not see how I was attached...'

This report is astonishingly similar to one which I cited as part of an OBE in

Wassermann (1993, p. 54 case 7). As cited by Myers (1892, p. 194) in the latter OBE, the Rev. L.J. Bertrand thought 'Well, at last I am what they call a dead man, and here I am, *a ball of air in the air*, a captive balloon still attached to earth by a kind of elastic string up and always up.'

In the preceding two OBE reports we have again some of the *class characteristics* of OBEs, namely that the OBEr sees (in many or most, perhaps all cases) his own body from the outside, that the OBEr experiences upward floating. The *elastic cord* cited in the Bertrand case is also a *class characteristic* of some OBEs (see Wassermann, 1993 for an extensive discussion of the cord).

Again, consider the following case cited by Lazarus (1993, p. 165). The case concerns a young army doctor

'who was involved in a biplane crash in April 1916. As the fuselage disintegrated on impact around him, he felt his physical body seemingly torn apart. However, the sensation of pain and panic was momentary. Seconds later he found himself floating high above the airfield, very much alive and apparently unhurt. Though confused, the doctor was also strangely detached and calm as he witnessed frantic attempts *on the ground to revive his own body*. Without knowing how, he abruptly returned to his natural state when an ambulance man began to pour a stimulant down his throat.'

In this case also we have a *floating high above the airfield being experienced by the percipient*.

The preceding OBE, reported by Broughton (1991) was earlier also reported by Celia Green (1976, p. 112).

In my own theory (Wassermann, 1993) I have postulated that normal conscious cognitive processes are mediated by the shadow matter brain and not by the ordinary matter brain. By contrast, it was postulated that in an OBE the shadow matter brain (which, by hypothesis, is normally attached to the ordinary matter brain) becomes partly or wholly detached from the ordinary matter brain. When this happens the shadow matter brain can still function normally and (via shadow matter eyes) perceive the world as in normal visual perception (etc.), and represent reality as in normal perception.

Consciousness & Near Death Experiences 25

Another relevant case history is cited by Blackmore (1993, pp. 164–167). It is too long to be fully repeated here, and I shall only cite a few particularly significant excerpts, leaving the reader to look up the full case history in Blackmore's book. In June 1944 an army corporal while accidentally grasping a 'live' open-ended supply plug (with 250 volts) received a massive and sustained shock which lasted until the plug was removed by others. The percipient noted that

> 'although unable to see, hear or move as the current surged through me to earth I was still able to think. Then suddenly I was *floating above my body* linked to it by what appeared to be a *shimmering cord.* I was *looking down on myself* laying in the grass. . . . I was quite peaceful floating some 15 feet above. . .'

Here, once more, we have some of the *'classic' class characteristics* of OBEs, some of which occurred also in some of the other OBE cases cited above. There is the *upward floating,* the *'seeing by the percipient of his own body below* on the grass (i.e. *seeing his body from the outside*) and also *the cord* which links the floating percipient with his body below. This is similar to the elastic cord experienced by the percipient in the third OBE reported above (the case of Rev. Bertrand).

Or, let me give an excerpt from one of Moody's (1976, p. 37) OBE cases, to show that OBE case histories coming from widely different sources may exhibit some of the same (multiple) *class characteristics.* This case concerned a car crash in which the percipient was involved. The percipient reported:

> 'I heard this awful sound—the side of the car being crushed in—and there was just an instant during which I seemed to be going through a darkness, *an enclosed space.* . . Then I was *floating* about five feet *above* the street, about five yards away from the car, . . . I could *see my own body* in the wreckage among all those people and could see them trying to get it out. . . .'

Here again we have some of the same *class characteristics.* The passing through an enclosed space is *not* typical of an OBE, but appears to be similar to the passing through a 'dark tunnel' reported in many general NDEs of which OBEs may be component aspects. But the experienced floating above the street, and the seeing of one's own body from the outside are again typical of other OBEs. Significantly, this case indicates how closely other than OBE aspects of the NDE (i.e. the dark tunnel) are related to an OBE in some cases.

Those OBE percipients who experience upward floating, form a subclass of OBE percipients with *repeatable class characteristics*. There are various other repeatable *class characteristics* of various OBEs; see some of the examples cited above). Many people who are or were unfamiliar with OBEs, NDEs etc. (e.g. presumably the late Sir Karl Popper) have not appreciated the kind of repeatability here under discussion and its importance.

Thus Popper (in Popper and Eccles 1977, p. 117) claimed that the results of parapsychology 'are not reproducible'. This is a deplorable mix-up of repeatedly discovered *class characteristics* of spontaneous psychic phenomena (e.g. many OBEs) and non-reproducibility of results 'to order' in repetitions of certain experiments (see also Wassermann, 1993 p. 61). (But see Radin (1997 pp. 36ff).)

In Moody's idealized 'composite' account of a NDE, cited above, an OBE formed a significant component. What is one to make of a typical OBE, i.e. how can one explain it? In my recent book (W93) I provided already a fully mechanistic theory of OBEs within the framework of a wider mechanistic theory of psi-phenomena.

Later in this book I shall present a somewhat improved version of my earlier theory of OBEs, which now also explains in terms of a modified version of Archimedes' principle the upward floating experienced by many OBE percipients. While my kinds of explanations are fully physicalistic and mechanistic, this does not apply to the explanations of OBEs suggested by Blackmore (1993 pp. 173 ff). So let me examine Blackmore's theory in shortened form

1.7 Critique of Blackmore's Theory of OBEs

Blackmore (1993, p.173) assumes that people, with the help of their brains, construct *models of reality*. She writes:

> 'The normal model of reality is based on sensory information of two main kinds. Firstly there is all the information coming in to the brain from the outside

through the ears, nose, eyes, skin and so on. From this a model of the world is built up that serves very well for us to get around. It appears detailed, accurate and comprehensive but in fact we know a lot of it is invented; gaps are filled in and plausible bits are created.'

The notion that we build models via internal representations has long been popular, notably since the Gestalt psychologists. The idea suffered somewhat of a setback when various theorists assumed, probably very questionably, that the brain is, and acts like, a kind of computer. In fact, in W93 and in this book (see below) I assume that there exists not just the brain, but, in addition, a *Shadow Matter brain* made up of Shadow Matter (as stipulated and described in W93). According to my previous (and present) theory it is not the ordinary matter brain which performs cognitive acts, such as memorizing, thinking, imagining and so forth. Rather it is the Shadow Matter brain, which performs and represents all of these cognitive acts, including model building of 'reality'.

Blackmore postulates that in an OBE the ordinary matter brain's model of reality breaks down. In particular she assumes that it is just the various means which are known to induce OBEs, for instance certain drugs which she lists (Blackmore, 1993, p. 176), that help to break down the model of reality. She sums up her view (l.c. p. 177) thus:

'At last we have a simple theory of the OBE. The normal model of reality breaks down and the system tries to get back to normal by building a new model from memory and imagination. If this model is in a bird's-eye view, then an OBE takes place.'

Blackmore's theory would be convincing and elegant if it explained the facts. But it does not. In particular it does not explain the *class characteristics* of OBEs listed above, although Blackmore (1993, pp. 177 ff) claims that her theory does explain these (or some of these) characteristics. To me the central difficulty of her view as follows. Suppose different people with differently endowed cognitive systems (e.g. different memories, different types of imagination etc.) experience an alleged breakdown of their 'model of reality'. Then all of them are supposed to produce just one or the other of the typical *class characteristics* of an OBE.

In my opinion, that just these, and not totally different breakdown symptoms happen seems implausible. I conclude that Blackmore's theory of the OBE does not explain the OBE at all.

Typically Blackmore (1993, p. 177–178) claims that her theory 'certainly explains why the OBE seems so real. It is real in the same sense that anything is ever real. That is the new OB model of reality is the best the system has at the time.'

I believe that in order to *explain* why the OBE is real one needs first a theory that explains how in normal perception things appear real. Such a theory has to be formulated in terms of appropriate brain (or Shadow Matter brain) mechanisms. At present no mechanism of the ordinary matter brain, or the postulated Shadow Matter brain (of Wassermann, 1993) provides any mechanisms that could represent reality in *normal* perception or in OBEs (or in other NDE phenomena).

I believe, therefore, that Blackmore's claim to have 'explained' the reality nature (or feeling) of the OBE is entirely spurious. On p. 178 of her book Blackmore (1993) also lists some of the OBE features that need explaining, and which will be explained later in this book, and which Blackmore, in my opinion, has not genuinely explained. She writes

> 'There are many other details that need explaining. There are the sensations of leaving, the fact that the double nearly always seems to be above the physical looking down, its transparency and ability to travel. There is the fact that many OBErs do not have a double at all but simply seem to be looking from a new position in space. There is the appearance of the world in this state, with the added ability to see through things, round corners and long distances. Any theory must also be able to account for when and why the OBE occurs: what is there about relaxing or meditating at home, taking a driving test or riding a motor bike for long hours that is in common with nearly dying? Finally there are the claims that people when OB see things they could not possibly have known about. . . .'

Various of these OBE features just listed have already been explained in terms of my postulated Shadow Matter theory, given in Wassermann (1993). This appeared about the same time as Blackmore's (1993) book. Probably she could not have known about my new theory at the time she was writing her book. Also, my theory of Wassermann (1993), as far as OBEs are concerned, (and NDEs), will be extended later in this book and will also be partly repeated.

1.8 The 'Afterlife Hypothesis' and Mechanistic Materialism

Now let me turn to Chapter 13 of Blackmore's (1993) book. She writes

'It is time now to return to the major question. Which hypothesis best accounts for the evidence: the 'Afterlife Hypothesis' or the 'Dying Brain Hypothesis'? Are NDEs a glimpse of life after death or the vision of a dying brain?'

I think that this question is obviously wrongly posed. I have repeatedly drawn attention to the fact (and so has Dr. Fenwick) that NDEs can also occur when brains are not dying. For this reason I reject the 'Dying Brain Hypothesis' as inadequate and opt for the 'Afterlife Hypothesis'. Yet, I should like to stress two points. First, in the later parts of this book as in chapter 5 of Wassermann (1993) it will be made clear that accepting, the 'Afterlife Hypothesis' does not mean abandoning mechanistic materialism. On the contrary, all my arguments regarding psi-phenomena, including OBEs and possible (and perhaps likely) survival, were based on a strictly mechanistic materialistic foundation.

The occurrence of all psi-phenomena, including survival, was explained entirely in terms of *mechanisms* (ordinary matter, as known to physicists and Shadow Matter which has also recently been postulated by physicists (Kolb *et al* (1985)) in *Nature*. I shall, however, have to enhance considerably the theory of Wassermann (1993) in order to deal with NDEs. Second, in order to strengthen the 'Afterlife Hypothesis', considerably, I shall have to consider evidence beside NDEs. For this purpose I shall, later in this book, consider *reincarnation phenomena*, notably those studied by the eminent parapsychologist Professor Ian Stevenson, who is the leading authority on this topic. (He is Carson Professor of Psychiatry in the Division of Personality Studies, Health Science Center, University of Virginia, Charlottesville VA 22908 US.)

Dr. Blackmore, by not considering reincarnation phenomena at all, failed to provide her readers with a truely comprehensive account of the total evidence that seems to point to the validity of the 'Afterlife Hypothesis'. What is at fault are not just the numerous apparent errors in her interpretations but her total panoramic view of the total evidence for the 'Afterlife Hypothesis'.

Let me now ask: if there is an afterlife then what is it that survives? Later in this book I shall argue (as in Wassermann 1993) that a human being consists of an ordinary material body. To this is bound among other things a *material soul* (a view already held by some materialist Greek philosophers of antiquity). At death the material soul (not to be confused with the immaterial soul of Cartesian interaction dualist philosophers) becomes detached from the physical body. When that physical body decays or is cremated the material soul or Shadow Matter brain remains intact. It is assumed to be the carrier of our memories, of our cognitive faculties and our consciousness both when we are alive and when we survive death. The matter of the soul, according to this view, is not ordinary matter, but a variant of *Shadow Matter* to be discussed later and the soul is to be equated with the Shadow Matter brain.

Among those writers of antiquity who put forward the notion of a material soul is Philo. Bowker (1991, p. 64) writes 'The Jewish writer who makes an even more explicit and deliberate attempt to interpret Judaism in terms which make real connection with the Greek imagination is, of course, Philo. However much Philo may later have been disowned by Judaism, at the time when he was alive he was by no means alone in remaining (as he emphatically believed) faithful to Torah, while interpreting Torah in terms established in Greek philosophy. . . .' Again, Bowker (l.c. p. 65) noted that Philo 'argued more than once that the soul of man is material, and that it is made of a fifth substance, *aether*, the fifth substance being different from the four elements of a body.'

This is historically interesting from my point of view. Like Philo (though obviously not in terms of his now hopelessly dated ideas about matter) I believe that the material soul is made of a kind of matter which differs in kind from the matter that makes up the ordinary matter body, namely *Shadow Matter* (see Wassermann, 1993 and below).

Turning now to further views by Blackmore (1993, p. 260) we note that she claims that her arguments 'are now strong enough to take on the challenge offered by many NDE investigators. Melvin Morse (1990) claims that 'There is no scientific explanation for the light', Michael Talbot refers to 'the inability of our current scientific understanding of reality even to begin to explain NDEs' (Talbot, 1991,

p. 244), and philosopher and parapsychologist Michael Grosso has said that "Explaining NDEs is obviously a large undertaking. The most that can be said now is that they cannot be adequately accounted for by any of the reductionist theories" (Grosso, 1981).'

Blackmore's theory, as we have seen (in the light of the criticisms of Fenwick and some of my own criticisms) cannot explain most of the NDE. But there are alternative approaches possible (Wassermann, 1993 and below) which offer, perhaps, a somewhat more optimistic outlook. Let me first of all consider Talbot's (1991) passage cited above. The possibility exists that our feeling of reality of something could be an epiphenomenon of some process of the ordinary matter brain (or possibly of the Shadow Matter brain, see Wassermann, 1993) does not exclude our partial scientific understanding of what brains (and perhaps Shadow Matter brains) do. Thus, if we cannot explain the nature of certain epiphenomena of normal perception, this does not necessarily rule out our partial explanation of NDEs.

1.9 Reality and the Shadow Matter Brain

Let me cite Vernon, in a passage which I cited already in Wassermann (1994, p. 140). Vernon (1952, p. 191) wrote

> 'Michotte (1950) considers... that although we may acquire knowledge about the nature of 'reality' through learning from experience, yet we have a primary fundamental, direct, and unanalyzable impression of 'reality'. This impression that a thing is 'real' can be differentiated from our knowledge or belief in its 'reality'. For instance in the cinema we receive the impression that the movements of objects on the screen are 'real' movements, although we know in fact that they are merely a succession of images in different spatial positions. Again, in ordinary life we spontaneously distinguish between an object which is 'real' and a picture of that object which is not. Michotte has attempted to investigate what are the conditions leading to this direct impression of 'reality'.'

I suggested (in W93), that there exist two interlinked brains in man (and, presumably, also in higher animals), first an ordinary matter brain, as described by anatomists and other life scientists. In addition, there is a Shadow Matter brain, whose constituents are composed of Shadow Matter in the way proposed in

(W93). Cognitive experiences, including the experience of reality could have their physical representations located in the Shadow Matter brain (which is the equivalent of a material soul or part of it) and not in the ordinary matter brain. If during an OBE the Shadow Matter brain becomes detached from the ordinary matter brain, then all cognitive faculties would remain *localized* in, and move with, the Shadow Matter brain.

As the Shadow Matter body and its Shadow Matter brain move about in space, during the OBE, the faculty to think and perceive spatially (via the Shadow Matter eyes, cf. W93), would move about with, and remain linked to, the Shadow Matter brain. In particular this would apply to the assumed shadow-matter-brain-located representation of reality. Hence, according to this view, the world perceived in an OBE, though differently located in relation to the experiencer, would be represented (and epiphenomenally experienced) as real as the world before the onset of the OBE.

There are people who, like C.J.S. Clarke (1995), believe that consciousness (or mentality) is nonlocalized. This, however, is a purely metaphysical belief, which is here opposed by the equally metaphysical belief that mentality is localized, namely, in the Shadow Matter brain. I think that one of the main reasons for putting forward the localized mentality hypothesis, rather than Clarke's (1995) hypothesis of nonlocality, is based on the explanation of OBEs by the locality hypothesis. The nonlocality thesis seems to furnish no such explanations. In fact, Clarke does not mention or discuss OBEs in his paper. Conceivably, in the face of overwhelming evidence, based on findings of NDEs, he may not believe that NDEs or OBEs exist.

Thus, *pace* Talbot (1991), we can understand, if we wish to do so, reality in its appearance in normal perception and in OBEs in terms of the Shadow Matter brain theory postulated in Wassermann (1993). These notions do not clash with current science, although they go beyond it. What seems to be questionable, in my opinion, is the alleged 'inability of our current scientific understanding of reality'. It remains a scientific hypothesis that mentality, and with it our sense of reality, when it occurs, is localized in the Shadow Matter brain. The latter can, depending on conditions, remain either attached to the ordinary matter brain or move about in space, when it becomes detached from the ordinary matter brain.

When the Shadow Matter brain is attached to the ordinary matter brain, as is assumed to be normally the case (but not in an OBE), then it would be far from obvious to decide that mentality is bound to the ordinary matter brain. Epiphenomenalism would be compatible with alternatives, since epiphenomenalism assumes essentially that mentality is a byproduct of matter. Epiphenomenalism does not state what type of matter mentality is a byproduct of. Mentality could be a byproduct of the ordinary matter brain, or it could be a byproduct of the postulated Shadow Matter brain. As I argued in Wassermann (1993), OBEs are more readily reconcilable and explicable in terms of the latter of the two alternatives just cited.

After Talbot's declaration, Blackmore (1993, p. 261) mentions that philosopher and parapsychologist Michael Grosso has said that 'Explaining NDEs is obviously a large undertaking. The most that can be said now is that they cannot be adequately accounted for by any of the reductionist theories' (Grosso, 1981 p. 23).' This doctrinary statement, however, which seems to be very sweeping, need not be accepted. The introduction into physics of Shadow Matter by Kolb *et al.* (1985), and my subsequent use of it in parapsychology, is reductionist. It tries to stay entirely within the mechanistic materialistic framework, by adding to existing matter a new kind of matter, namely Shadow Matter by postulating for Shadow Matter specific properties, one does just as one postulates specific properties for ordinary matter in physics and chemistry (etc.).

1.10 Blackmore's Arguments against the Afterlife Hypothesis

It is, of course, easy to argue, as K. Ring (1982, p. 216) does, (cited by Blackmore (1993, p. 260)) that those who put their bets on neurological explanations of NDEs should explain neurologically such things as the OBE state, 'paranormal knowledge, the tunnel, the golden light, the voice or presence, the appearance of deceased relatives, beautiful vistas, and so forth'. If they have not succeeded in explaining this host of phenomena, then it does not follow that these phenomena cannot be explained in mechanistic materialistic terms. It may only mean that neurological explanations may not be the suitable means for explaining them. In fact, I have shown already (in W93) that many aspects of OBEs can be explained mechanistically, but not neurologically, in terms of Shadow Matter theory (see also Wassermann, 1988).

In four final arguments Blackmore (1993, pp. 261–263) tries to demolish arguments that are commonly used as evidence for the Afterlife Hypothesis. She, apparently, believes that by liquidating the Afterlife Hypothesis one can fortify the 'Dying Brain Hypothesis'. This, however, is not necessarily the case, since, for argument's sake, both hypotheses could be invalid, although I would place my bet on the acceptance of the metaphysical Afterlife Hypothesis.

The first argument which Blackmore tries to liquidate is the 'consistency' argument. 'This is that NDEs are similar around the world and throughout history'. Accordingly the OBE and the dark tunnel (etc.), are real and not just symptoms of the breakdown of a mental model of reality. Blackmore claims 'that the consistency is there but this does not mean there is an afterlife.' Instead, she believes that the consistency is due to corresponding abnormal ways of actions by different brains in the process of producing similar NDEs. Thus, in accordance with what I mentioned earlier in this chapter, she claims that 'The OBE is consistent because it is the brain's way of dealing with the breakdown in the body image and model of reality.'

The trouble with these arguments is that, as Fenwick (1994), in his critique of Blackmore's theory, and I, in my criticisms of her interpretations of OBEs, have suggested, Blackmore's theory, in particular her views on OBEs, is invalid. As far as I know, Blackmore has not validly rebutted these criticisms. Undoubtedly, I have vested interests, because I am proposing in this book completely different explanations of NDEs (and OBEs, see also Wassermann, 1993). But Blackmore places, for example, strong emphasis on the role played by endorphins in producing the 'life review' (according to which in a flash a percipient of a NDE can experience a very rapid review of many events of his/or her past life). But, as shown above, Fenwick (1994) has emphatically repudiated the role allocated by her to the endorphins, and I have not come across any convincing counter arguments.

Thus, the dying brain hypothesis does not account adequately for NDEs. Contrary to this, Blackmore (1993, p. 261) claims that 'No afterlife hypothesis is required to account for the consistency of NDEs across times, peoples and cultures. Indeed the dying brain hypothesis accounts for it better.' I believe that in the preceding quotation Blackmore appears to misunderstand basic notions in the philosophy of science. Certainly, no hypothesis in any part of science can be shown to be necessary, else it would not be a hypothesis. Thus that the afterlife hypothesis is not necessary does not imply that it could not be sufficient. Blackmore, it seems, is simply confusing necessity and sufficiency.

Another argument in favour of an afterlife, which Blackmore (l.c. p. 261-262) tries to rebut, is, what she terms, the 'reality argument'. This argument claims 'that NDEs feel so real that they must be what they appear to be, a real journey to the next world.' Blackmore (l.c. p. 262) argues that 'All we have is model-building and we call some models 'real' and some 'imaginary'. The most stable and persistent ones, like those based on the senses, we call real.' . . . 'Mostly this works well but during the NDE it leads us astray. Stable tunnel forms in the cortex seem real. An out of the body perspective taken on in imagination seems real. So the felt 'realness' of NDEs is no evidence that there is anyone to travel out of the body or any next world to go to. The dying brain hypothesis thus accounts better for why the experience seems real and can also account for why obviously 'unreal' things are seen in NDEs as well.'

I do not think any of Blackmore's preceding arguments are valid. Her assumption that the 'tunnel' is a creation of the dying cerebral cortex seems to me unfounded and lacking in any evidence and, thus as completely metaphysical as some opposing interpretations. Indeed, later in this book I shall argue that the tunnel genuinely exists as a material tunnel and is not created as a phantasm of the dying brain. Likewise, I have argued (Wassermann, 1993), and shall do so again, that OBEs are real and correspond to real transactions of real material (Shadow Matter) systems, and that OBEs are not creations of the imagination. Accordingly the dying brain hypothesis does not account as well for NDEs as alternative hypotheses which allocate reality to such things as the tunnel and OBEs. It is for these reasons that I reject, once more, Blackmore's favoured hypothesis of the 'dying brain'.

Next, Blackmore examines what she terms the 'paranormal argument' According to her this argument asserts that NDEs 'involve paranormal events which cannot be explained by science. Since they cannot be explained in any normal way they must be evidence that the NDE involves another dimension, another world, or the existence of a non-material spirit or soul.'

Now, none of these arguments are valid. *Pace* Blackmore, paranormal events, including OBEs, *can* be explained by science, although the explanations may involve very recent scientific notions, such as *Shadow Matter*, first advanced in the leading scientific journal *Nature* by Kolb *et al.* (1985). Thus pace Blackmore, OBEs and NDEs can (see chapter 3 below), in principle, be explained scientifically, without invoking 'another dimension, another world, or the existence of non-material spirits or souls'. While all this is not necessarily an argument for an afterlife, it is, in terms of the theory of Wassermann (1993), and of the present book, compatible with an afterlife.

Blackmore states that she (1993, p. 262) has cast considerable doubt on the evidence for paranormal phenomena. 'Many cases are simply very weak to start with, others become weaker the deeper you look into them and some have even been invented altogether.' . . . 'If the evidence changes in the future and truely convincing paranormal events are documented then certainly the theory I have proposed will have to be overthrown—along with a lot more of psychology, physics and biology . . .'.

To start with, I do not think that many, or most, people who are familiar with current parapsychology (e.g. Bem and Honorton, 1994, Radin, 1997) will accept the sweeping generalizations by Blackmore (1993, p. 262). They will not believe that there is considerable doubt about the evidence of paranormal phenomena. Blackmore is entitled to entertain such feeble beliefs. (In fact the important experiments of Bem and Honorton (1994) and Radin's (1997) important book were published after Blackmore's (1993) book, and Blackmore may not have been aware of this work.) I have elsewhere surveyed and discussed some of the evidence for spontaneous psychic phenomena (Wassermann, 1993). Also, it does not follow that if we accept the evidence for psi-phenomena (e.g. the experimental Ganzfeld work of Bem and Honorton (1994) and Morris and others and the many spontaneous cases discussed by Wassermann (1993)) that we have to 'overthrow' much of psychology, physics and biology.

I have argued in terms of a purely physicalistic theory, which is compatible with psychology, physics and biology, that psi-phenomena are compatible with phenomena of ordinary sciences. I simply believe that Blackmore lacks familiarity with physics although I could be mistaken. *Pace* Blackmore (1993), I have provided massive counter-examples against her generalizations (Wassermann, 1993), which seem to me unfounded. The fact that Blackmore has had little luck in detecting or experiencing many psi-phenomena (but not OBEs, see Blackmore (1982)) does not mean that other people were not luckier, or, as regards OBEs, equally lucky (cf. Green, (1968)). I do not think that anything is as bad and risky in science as to make sweeping generalizations of the kind Blackmore engages in.

After her rhetoric concerning the paranormal, Blackmore (1993, p. 262) proclaims that:

'the dying brain hypothesis explains why people seek paranormal evidence to bolster their impression of realness and how the stories are passed on and elaborated. By understanding the role of the limbic system and temporal lobe it accounts for the experiences of familiarity, insight and *déjà vu* and for the increase of psychic experiences after the NDE. I shall keep looking for the evidence that might prove it wrong but for now the dying brain hypothesis accounts better for what we know.'

Admittedly, if one does not attempt to explain the details of the OBE and, with it, of NDEs, then Blackmore's argument might seem spuriously convincing. Likewise her tirade against the paranormal might superficially convince those who do not know any better. Particularly those who have not had a thorough grounding in the philosophy of science.

Following the various arguments listed and discussed, Blackmore (1993, p. 263) cites the 'transformation argument'. 'This is that people are changed by their NDEs, sometimes dramatically for the better, becoming more spiritual and less materialistic.' What, precisely, Blackmore means here by 'materialistic' is not clear to me, although I consider myself as a mechanistic materialist (see, Wassermann, 1994). Admittedly the 'afterlife hypothesis' cannot explain this, and the reasons why the 'dying brain hypothesis' can supposedly explain the 'transformation' leave me unconvinced, once more, as do so many of Blackmore's spurious arguments.

Towards the end of her long, and, I believe, often mistaken, arguments Blackmore (1993, p. 263) concludes:

'All things considered, I can see no reason to adopt the afterlife hypothesis. I am sure I shall remain in the minority for a long time to come, especially among NDErs, but for me the evidence and the arguments are overwhelming. The dying brain hypothesis, for all its shortcomings does a better job of accounting for the experiences themselves. And it reveals not a false hope of the self surviving for ever but a genuine insight beyond the self.'

Let me remind readers that the cardinal weakness with the dying brain hypothesis is the fact that various people who have had NDEs were not dying, so that they did not have a dying brain.

Possibly Blackmore does not appreciate that the 'afterlife hypothesis', unlike the dying brain hypothesis, is not intended to provide a scientific explanation of the NDE. For the latter kind of explanation the reader will have to turn to chapter 3 below and elsewhere in this book. Suffice it to state at this stage of the book that if there exists an afterlife, then this is consistent with a physicalistic, mechanistic materialistic explanation of the NDE. Indeed, readers who have sampled my book *Shadow Matter And Psychic Phenomena* will have seen that OBEs do not require an afterlife hypothesis for their explanations. The further explanations of OBEs, and tunnels given in chapter 3 below will reinforce this conclusion.

1.11 The Directivity (or Purpose) of Life

In the final paragraph of her book, Blackmore (1993, p. 263–264) writes:

> 'We are biological organisms, evolved in fascinating ways for no purpose at all and with no end in any mind. We are simply here and that is how it is. I have no self and 'I' own nothing. There is no one to die. There is just this moment, and now this and now this.'

This passage by Blackmore may, however, be a great act of self-deception of a disbeliever in a hereafter. If we survive (as Shadow Matter bodies) then our abilities to think and remember, survive with our Shadow Matter brain. Although our ordinary matter bodies do not survive, our surviving entities may develop further in the hereafter and produce great new intellectual improvements and achievements for certain surviving personalities.

Blackmore's opinion that 'we are biological organisms, evolved in fascinating ways for no purpose at all and with no end in any mind' probably is, totally wrong. (Cf. my book Wassermann, 1997, particularly my paper 'On the Nature of the Theory of Evolution' reproduced in Wassermann 1997 and previously published in *Philosophy Of Science*). One of the main features of evolutionary theory is the aim of explaining the nature of adaptations, which may *simulate* purposefulness.

For instance, consider so-called pseudo-exogenous adaptations (Wassermann, 1997). One typical example of these occurs in the ostrich. The ostrich develops on its underside callosities just where it touches the ground when squatting. At first sight it looks as if the callosities are due to the effects of the ground on the underside of the animal. But this is not so! The callosities are present at birth and form prior to this during development as a result of genetic control, although the genes involved are unknown. Various other kinds of pseudo-exogenous adaptations are known for various kinds of animals, and they all simulate purposefulness. In fact, purpose itself, in human beings, could be produced by specifically adapted brain parts. The adaptations involved could in many cases be of the pseudo-exogenous variety, by one part of a brain adapting to another appropriate part (with similar remarks for the Shadow Matter brain).

The view that all kinds of adaptations in animals and plants evolve only subject to combined random mutations and natural selection without directivity in the evolutionary processes seems misguided. Genetic changes certainly play a central role in evolutionary processes, but one cannot conclude that many or most of these are random changes of genes.

Following Mekler (1967) and Cook (1977) I helped to develop a new paradigm which explains how environmental stress (as e.g. in the ostrich example cited above) could lead to the directed evolution of appropriate genes. Once evolved, these could lead, during development, to the formation of novel kinds of organs and/or structures. I called this new paradigm template induced molecular adaptation, or TIMA for short (see Wassermann 1982a for TIMA part1, 1982b for TIMA part2 and 1997 for TIMA part 3). TIMA, in fact, provides postulated molecular biological machinery for simulating directed adaptive processes (or, if you prefer, 'purposeful' adaptive processes).

To remind readers of the, often, extreme intricacy of adaptations, I wish to refer them to Huxley's (1942) book *Evolution: The modern Synthesis*. Among numerous important examples Huxley mentions the following one (op. cit. p. 427).

'The giant panda (*Ailuropoda melanoleuca*) has recently been shown to possess an unexpected structural adaptation to its special feeding habits (Wood-Jones 1939). As is well known, this aberrant carnivore lives almost exclusively on bambooshoots. In order to hold these properly while feeding, the sesamoid bone on the radial side of the hand has been much enlarged and furnished with a regular articulation with the scaphoid bone, and a muscle which normally runs to the base of the pollex has become diverted to it. The sesamoid with its overlying horny pad has thus become modified into an organ functioning as an opposable thumb. The actual pollex was apparently too specialized to be modified in this direction. Through this remarkable adaptation the giant panda has become endowed with delicate grasping capacity far beyond that of any other member of the order, though the common panda (*Ailurus fulgens*) shows some modification in this direction.'

In my opinion Blackmore (1993), in the final paragraph of her book, trivializes the immensely subtle adaptations that occur in nature (cf. the preceding example). For instance the human skull neatly fits the underlying soft tissues and, indirectly, neatly fits the brain. The rib cage indirectly neatly fits the lungs, and many millions of similar examples are familiar to biologists. Even coadaptations in male and female occur in the sex organs. Thus, the erect human penis fits the vagina. Although, to cite Blackmore, there 'is no end in mind', the evolutionary and developmental mechanisms that lead to these intricate structures carry on as if they are goal-directed. To attribute all this to chance rather than to ordered mechanisms (such as my postulated TIMA machinery, Wassermann, 1982a, 1982b, 1997, 1999) seems to me unwarranted.

Our life span, which is maximally species-specific, seems to be genetically controlled. In fact, if all humans, animals and plants lived indefinitely then our planet would become overcrowded with living creatures and would not be able to sustain them.

From the preceding part of this chapter we may conclude that the dying brain theory for explaining the NDE and related phenomena is not viable, at least in the version developed by Blackmore. The fact that NDEs occur also in people who are not dying at all, makes the 'dying brain hypothesis' a dubious proposition from the start. That, despite this, Blackmore tried to develop that kind of theory is very surprising. Nevertheless, although Fenwick's rebuttal of Blackmore's theory is useful, it is no substitute for a theory that works.

1.12 Jansen's Approach to the NDE

Another interesting, criticism permeates Fenwick's discussion of R.I. Jansen's (1996) theory of the NDE, to which I shall now turn. Dr. Peter Fenwick, who was a consultant neuropsychiatrist at the Maudsley Hospital, London, was kind enough to send me his critical debate of Jansen's article. Fenwick's (1996) critique will be published in the *Journal of Near Death Experiences.*

In his article Fenwick (1996) notes that:

'Dr. Jansen argues, correctly in my view, that a clear sensorium and a feeling of absolute reality do not negate the suggestion that these experiences are hallucinations. From a scientific point of view it is clear that the majority of the NDE experiences must be hallucinations, if one excludes those out of body experiences for which a veridical nature is claimed, as the world described is private to the individual and not held in common between subjects. The fact that we define the NDE mainly as an hallucination is of little help either in terms of the experience's likely genesis or of its philosophical explanation.' . . .

Pace Fenwick, I do not accept the hypothesis that the NDE, or parts of it, is, or are, a hallucination. For instance, why should out-of-the-body experiences (OBEs) that occur in NDEs mostly, or perhaps always, involve, as a result of a hallucination, that the subject sees his, or her, own body from outside that body. Surely the subject could hallucinate myriads of quite different types of experiences. So why are in an OBE allegedly just such particular experiences hallucinated? Or, again, why do in so many OBEs of NDEs subjects experience that they are rising in space (see above), when these subjects could, instead, have hallucinated a multitude of totally different experiences?

I do not think that Fenwick has resolved this issue. Similar questions can be raised for the tunnel experience of the NDE, which, again, cannot, in any obvious way, be explained as a hallucination. Similar remarks apply to other aspects of the NDE. I shall suggest in Chapter 3, how several NDE phenomena can be explained in terms of the Shadow Matter theory, which I developed in my earlier book (W93) in order to explain numerous kinds of psi-phenomena.

I argued already in (W93) that hallucinations are inadequate to explain various kinds of psi-phenomena. I doubt whether Dr. Fenwick has seen my anti-hallucination hypothesis of (W93). The essence of these arguments is that in NDEs and, particularly, in OBEs, there occur *repeatable class characteristics*. For instance, in every OBE there occurs the experience of viewing one's body from the outside. This, in fact, may be considered as a defining feature of an OBE. Also, in many, or most, OBEs there occurs an experience of upward floating while one is 'out of the body'. That precisely such, and other, class characteristics should be hallucinated by subject after subject in many places on earth, when an unlimited number of totally different types of hallucinations would be possible, seems to me incredible.

Before I proceed with Jansen's and Fenwick's views, I shall recapitulate some aspects of my Shadow Matter theory of psychic phenomena (W93). This may be relevant to the further discussion. My Shadow Matter (=SM) theory of psi-phenomena assumes that every human being (and, likewise, every other organism) consists of an ordinary matter body, as described in anatomy texts. To this is bound a SM body, composed of SM. To each constituent (e.g. atom, ion, molecule etc.) of an ordinary matter body there is, by hypothesis, bound a corresponding SM constituent of the SM body. For instance, to each quark of the ordinary matter body there is assumed to be bound a corresponding squark (made of SM and, hence differing from the quark) of the SM body. To each electron of the ordinary matter body there is assumed to be bound a selectron of the SM body (the selectron differing in composition from the electron).

This, in turn, ensures that to each molecule of the ordinary matter brain there is bound a corresponding smolecule (made of SM) of the SM brain. It is assumed (in W93) that parts, or the whole, of the SM body can become detached from the ordinary matter body and move away from the latter. It is also assumed that it is not (as usually assumed) the ordinary matter brain but the SM brain (normally attached to the ordinary matter brain) which is the seat of mentality. Hence our thoughts, feelings etc. are epiphenomena of our SM brains. Suppose that in special circumstances, such as OBEs or NDEs, our SM brain becomes partly, or completely, detached from the ordinary matter brain, then, as before, our seat of consciousness remains located in the SM brain and moves with the SM brain. Likewise, our ability to think, feel etc., moves with the SM brain.

The present theory therefore differs radically from Jansen's view 'that mind *arises* from neuronal activity, and that consciousness is *local* to brain processes (cited from Fenwick (1996)). Unlike Jansen I envisage that all cognitive and all

Consciousness & Near Death Experiences 43

conscious events are transacted in the SM brain. They are not transacted in the ordinary matter brain to which the SM brain is, by hypothesis, normally bound. The assumption that the NDE is produced by the SM brain is consistent with Fenwick's conclusion, based on a large sample of NDEs. Fenwick notes 'that NDEs judged entirely by their phenomenology occur in many different circumstances. Any theory which links the NDE only to brain catastrophe or to special brain physiological mechanisms must provide only a partial and limited explanation.'

Perhaps, as I prefer to put it more plainly, neurophysiology provides simply no explanation of the NDE and OBE at all. In particular, *pace* Jansen, I do not think that 'the NDE is the result of the blocking of the PCP site (PCP= a synthetic form of glutamate) on the NMDA receptor (NMDA = N-methyl-D-aspartate). It would, for instance, be difficult to understand how the blocking of a single kind of receptor should lead to the variety of class characteristics of the OBE which is often a component of the NDE. OBEs (and their class characteristics) occur also in subjects who have no NDE (cf. Blackmore 1986). To assume that these OBEs are also caused by the blockage of the NMDA receptor seems implausible. Likewise it is difficult to understand how precisely the class characteristics of NDEs, notably of their sub-component OBEs, should resemble mystical experiences, as suggested by Fenwick and Fenwick (1995).

If we take, for instance, an ordinary OBE (not linked to a NDE) that has occurred to a rider of a motor bicycle. According to my theory, the shaking about of the motor cyclist could lead to a separation (under stress) of the Shadow Matter brain and the ordinary matter brain, leading to the spatial separation of the two brains. How, precisely, do Fenwick and Fenwick (1995) or Jansen explain the resulting OBE? An explanation similar to the one of the OBE of a motor cyclist could explain why astronauts who are centrifuged at high speed have OBEs. Here too their Shadow Matter brain could, under stress, become partly or completely separated from their ordinary matter brain.

Fenwick (1996) asserts that 'The phenomenon of a clear sensorium in catastrophic brain states is more difficult to explain. Any physician dealing with head injury, epilepsy or altered cerebral physiology knows that as cerebral function becomes compromised it becomes disorganized. Even in such simple circumstances as ordinary fainting, recovery from the faint is recovery from a confusional process. Acute cerebral catastrophes result in confusion not clarity.'

Let us explain the NDE, in particular its OBE component, as partly, or always, involving a separation of the Shadow Matter brain from the Ordinary matter brain. Suppose that the Shadow Matter brain is the carrier of cognitive phenomena and the seat of consciousness. Then, the separated Shadow Matter brain in a NDE could still have conscious states corresponding to a clear sensorium, irrespective of whether the state of the ordinary matter brain (from which separation has occurred) is catastrophic or otherwise.

My type of theory simply envisages that OBEs and NDEs come about by mechanisms differing completely from the mechanisms envisaged by Fenwick (which only consider the ordinary matter brain). The hypothesis of the existence of Shadow Matter (as first invoked by Kolb *et al.* in *Nature* (London) (1985) in connection with 'dark matter' was not taken into account by Fenwick.

Fenwick (1996) stresses that Jansen... 'does not explain how NDE experiences can arise in a dysfunctional brain.' By contrast, my theory argues that these experiences do not arise in the dysfunctional ordinary matter brain at all (as both Jansen and Fenwick assume). They arise in the Shadow Matter brain, e.g. when the latter separates partly, or completely, from the ordinary matter brain.

As regards the plausibility of Shadow Matter within my theory (of Wassermann 1993) Nobel Laureate Professor Brian D. Josephson (Physics Cambridge), a Fellow of the Royal Society, wrote to me after sampling my 1993 Book *Shadow Matter And Psychic Phenomena.*

> 'The idea that some non-ordinary form of matter can explain psi is one I think may be worth following up, as you have done, in an attempt to get some way of thinking about these elusive phenomena. Purely as phenomenology your ideas may be very valuable.'

Returning to Fenwick's (1996) paper. He cites that 'we had patients who were head injured and whose arousal was confusional and showed all the characteristics and mental states that would be expected after a severe head injury. Yet within this dense confusional state, but attributed by the individual to the time of unconsciousness, was full memory of a wonderfully clear NDE.' This, again, could be explained by the Shadow Matter brain becoming detached from the ordinary matter brain as a result of the head injury.

However, during the time of detachement the Shadow Matter brain could lead to the wonderfully clear NDE, and remember it. When subsequent reunion of the Shadow Matter brain and the ordinary brain occurred, then normal Shadow Matter brain states could resurface. With them recall of the memory (Shadow Matter brain engrams) of the NDE, which then, via the ordinary matter brain and motor systems, could have led to a spoken account of the perceived NDE.

Those who are given to more traditional neuropsychological explanations of NDEs may well share Fenwick's (1996) different view that 'Except by special pleading it is not possible with our current understanding of cerebral functioning to explain on a simple chemical theory how within dense unconsciousness and with absence of memory the brain can structure and remember a clear comprehensive' [NDE] . . . Fenwick states that this conclusion 'is an interesting point and is a challenge to our current understanding of brain function. (Teasdale 1991, Cartlidge 1991).' Seen from the orthodox point of view of brain functioning this is certainly quite true. However, seen from the novel point of view of the ordinary brain and the postulated Shadow Matter brain one obtains a totally different picture and a way out of the orthodox puzzle. Also the clear memory for the NDE which puzzles orthodox brain scientists (see Fenwick, 1996) no longer poses a challenge in my model. The memory is now formed (i.e. any memory for anything) by the Shadow Matter brain and not by the ordinary matter brain. Hence, when the Shadow Matter brain becomes detached from the (grossly subfunctional) ordinary matter brain, engrams could be formed in the still functional Shadow Matter brain. This presumably *is* functional as witnessed by its assumed production of the NDE.

Much of Fenwick's article deals with what the NDE is unlikely to be and unlikely to be caused by. Among his many negativisms there is Fenwick's (1996) allegation, in an almost unknown journal that 'As yet we have no clear theory to explain parapsychological experiences.' Yet, *pace* Fenwick (1996) there is my very comprehensive (and, I believe, clear) theory of parapsychological phenomena (Wassermann, 1988, 1993) which he totally ignored. Perhaps he does not know enough modern physics to comprehend the theory of Kolb *et al* (1985), published in the leading scientific journal *Nature*. On this I based my Shadow Matter theory of psi-phenomena (Wassermann, 1988, 1993) of which Fenwick seems to be unaware. Psi-phenomena are no longer outside science, thanks to the Shadow

Matter theory of psi-phenomena. In fact, *pace* Fenwick (1996) who puts his explanatory bet on a hitherto undeveloped non-local theory of mind. Yet we can now rely on localized mentality which is localized in the Shadow Matter brain and which can explain normal thinking as well as thinking during psi-phenomena in similar terms (cf. Wassermann, 1993). I have published my Shadow Matter theory of psi-phenomena first in the prominent journal *Inquiry* (Wassermann, 1988). Again, Fenwick (1996) took no notice of it, simply denying that any clear current theory exists. The trouble is that most medical people know very little or no highly advanced modern physics of the type required for understanding Shadow Matter theory. This suggests why Fenwick simply ignored my work.

Equally debatable is Fenwick's (1996) remark that out-of-the-body experiences (OBEs) 'have a heterogeneous phenomenology. Some can quite easily be explained by current conventional science it suggests that the brain creates our subjective experience of our body and its position in space from sensory information.' This, however, does not explain the experienced floating in so many OBEs or the experience of seeing one's body from the outside, or why the body seems to be floating upwards.

At least in my book (Wassermann, 1993) I explained OBEs in detail. I have driven the theory further in the present book (Chapter 3). For instance, Fenwick (1996) writes that in an OBE 'the body is experienced as being elsewhere, for example on the ceiling, either for psychological reasons or because an alteration in brain physiology . . .'. This looks to me like a statement which lacks detailed mechanistic explanations (e.g. like those given in Wassermann (1993) or chapter 3 below). The fact that most of the floating in an OBE is upwards and not downwards cannot just be explained as being due to 'psychological reasons' or due to 'an alteration in brain physiology' Such explanations explain everything but nothing, since, e.g. the 'psychological reasons' could equally lead to a downward floating or to no floating at all. Again, Fenwick does not explain the nature of the apparently elastic cord which is experienced as connecting the ordinary matter body and the floating body (here identified as the Shadow Matter body).

I worked with Professor Herbert Fröhlich, FRS, near the time when he thought of his 'Fröhlich Oscillators' (when I was his Research assistant at Bristol University, 1947–1948). It cannot be denied that these oscillators (which were already known in solid state mechanics in similar form before that) could play a role in brains. It cannot be asserted that they do play a role, and what part exactly they play, if any. Here Fenwick seems to be using ideas from physics, perhaps unfamiliar to him, without showing us how they are to be applied in brain science. While he claims that these notions 'would support the idea of non-locality of mind' my notion of a Shadow Matter brain suggests that non-locality of mind may not be required.

Finally Fenwick states towards the end of his (1996) paper that 'some of the phenomena of the NDE suggest that subjective experience may be maintained in the face of severe cerebral catastrophe. If this is a possibility then the maintenance of subjective experience when brain function is severely disorganised has consequences for our understanding of brain processes and the nature of mind. It even raises the possibility that there might be a continuation of subjective experience after brain death.' Alas, Fenwick does not explain in detail how much of what he claims is possible could occur in mechanistic terms.

By contrast I explained some of this problematics. A detachable Shadow Matter brain, could be the carrier of subjective experience when that Shadow Matter brain is attached to the ordinary matter brain. Also in the out-of-the-body state the Shadow matter brain is detached from the ordinary matter brain. We can see that the Shadow Matter brain, when detached from the ordinary matter brain, can maintain subjective experience in the face of severe cerebral catastrophe of the ordinary matter brain. I have shown explicitly that this is a possibility. It has important consequences for understanding the mind-body problem (the mind being located in the Shadow Matter brain).

Also in Wassermann (1993) I suggested that at death the Shadow Matter body, and the Shadow Matter brain, could become detached from the ordinary matter body and ordinary matter brain, respectively. The Shadow Matter body and Shadow Matter brain could then survive destruction (e.g. by cremation) of the ordinary matter body and brain. The surviving Shadow Matter brain could then retain its engrams and its facilities to perform cognitive (etc.) functions. This, then provides an explicit view of what could happen, and such a view is missing from the end of Fenwick's (1996) paper.

Fenwick is, of course, right that 'our implicit everyday scientific assumptions in science do require questioning.' This is exactly what I have done in Wassermann (1993) and in this chapter and elsewhere in this book, by questioning whether the ordinary brain is really the carrier of mentality. I argued, instead that in addition to the ordinary brain there exists also a Shadow Matter brain which is normally attached to the ordinary matter brain and which is always the carrier of mentality. According to this, mentality is *localized* in the Shadow Matter brain.

Finally, *pace* Fenwick, I do not accept his claim that 'current science as formulated is not able to explain the implications of the NDE experience. Science is able to note brain correlates of the NDE where they exist, but cannot argue from these to the significance, or even the presence, of subjective experience.' This is only so if one thinks in terms of an 'ordinary brain only' model. If, however, one admits in addition the postulated existence of a Shadow Matter brain as carrier of mentality then one can argue to the *presence* of subjective experience in normal psychology *and* in NDEs. The secondary experiences, e.g. qualia etc., arise in my theory as epiphenomena of the functioning of the Shadow Matter brain. They can be activated in the same way when the Shadow Matter brain is either bound to the ordinary matter brain or when it is detached (as in OBEs). I am not claiming to explain secondary qualities in scientific terms. All I am claiming is the suggestion where the secondary qualities might be located (namely in the Shadow matter brain, where they occur as epiphenomena of Shadow Matter constituents). It can be seen that my theory is fully materialistic in the sense of Wassermann (1994). I shall return to these topics in Chapter 3.

1.13 Testability of the Shadow Matter Theory of paranormal Phenomena

It would not be surprising if some readers would ask 'is your theory of paranormal phenomena testable?' Although I have dealt with this topic in Wassermann (1993, p. 57–58) I shall repeat here what I have said there because of its importance.

> 'Although the present theory invokes several special assumptions (technically known as *ad hoc* hypotheses) for explaining each particular case history, this is really typical of most, if not all, scientific theories. I explained this elsewhere (Wassermann, 1994). In a typical scientific hypothetico-deductive theory, such as Newtonian Mechanics, one encounters hundreds, if not thousands, of systems to which the theory has been applied. In applying the general theory

to any particular system one requires particular assumptions special for that system only. In this case one says that the system is being 'modelled' by the general theory. For instance, in Newtonian Mechanics one may assume as an elementary system, that one has a 'smooth inclined plane' with a 'point particle' sliding down a line of greatest slope of the plane. Or a point particle may slide down a smooth, thin, circular wire located in a vertical plane. In this way one gets one system after another for which system-specific assumptions are being made, in addition to general 'laws' of mechanics (i.e. Newton's three 'laws' of motion). There is therefore nothing unusual when I introduce system-specific assumptions into my theory of psychic phenomena, in addition to general mechanisms which are used to explain many cases, and are applied to many different systems.'

'One way of testing my integrated theory of psi-phenomena is analogous to the way in which one has 'tested' many theories in physics. This is by using these theories to *explain* many already known phenomena, and by examining how these theories fit the phenomena. For instance, in 1905 Einstein explained the already known photo-electric effect, but did not predict it. His explanation also 'tested' Planck's earlier assumption of the existence and properties of light quanta (i.e. photons). Thus, Einstein explained the photo-electric effect by making assumptions about the properties of photons.

Likewise, the theory of superconductivity of Bardeen and his associates (e.g. Cooper) explained the already known phenomena of superconductivity, but did not predict them. [The late Professor Herbert Fröhlich contributed a key idea to the current theory of superconductivity [see his obituary in *The Times* (London) 30.1.1991 p. 16].] Again, Felix Bloch established a well known quantum theory of electronic conduction in metals, which explained many already known facts and laws (e.g. Ohm's Law) without predicting them. Einstein, Bardeen and Bloch (etc.) obtained Nobel Prizes for their respective explanatory feats listed, showing that explanations are highly valued in science, at least as much as valid predictions. Successful explanations serve as strong tests of a theory even if (like predictions) they cannot prove a theory to be true.'

My theory, as it stands, explains many already known phenomena of parapsychology and is, thus, severely tested by these explanations. It will be further severely tested by explanations of NDEs and of reincarnation. Another theory-linked test of my theory would be to demonstrate that some of its assumptions about Shadow Matter follow ultimately from a future 'Theory of Everything' (see Wassermann, 1993 p. 21) or are, at least, consistent with it. If so, as noted before (Wassermann, 1988 and Wassermann, 1993, p. 11) *psi-phenomena could provide the strongest indirect evidence for Shadow Matter* (as postulated in physics). Psi-phenomena [and NDEs] could help towards an important enlargement of the realm of mechanistic materialism, by giving Shadow Matter a firm footing.

2 Localized versus non-localized consciousness and mentality

2.1 The Heritage of Monotheism

Monotheism claims that there exists just one God, who is present everywhere, can apprehend everything anyone is doing, and, thus, is non-localized. As, according to some religions, God created man in his image, it has been assumed that the human 'mind' (whatever that may mean) is also non-localized and can be present everywhere. This, according to those who accept the non-localization of the human mind could account for telepathy as action at a distance. Telepathy, however, can range over more than a thousand kilometers. It seems somewhat difficult to envisage that everybody's mind should extend over more than a thousand kilometers and, yet, be anchored, somehow, to a narrowly located body.

Above all, what is the matter of the, presumably implied, material carrier that carries and extends the mind in a non-localized fashion? At any rate, the Shadow Matter brain, postulated and introduced by Wassermann (1988, 1993 and in the previous chapter) is assumed to be strictly localized. In normal circumstances, when it is assumed to be bound to the ordinary matter brain. In OBEs and NDEs when it is assumed to be detached from the ordinary matter brain. Also, by hypothesis (Wassermann 1993) the Shadow Matter brain is the seat of mentality.

Hence, Shadow Matter theory can dispense with the gratuitous hypothesis of a non-localized mind. Indeed it is a little hard to accept that the long-range carrier of psi-information should be bound to an ordinary matter brain, on the highly doubtful assumption of non-locality of mind'. Some people who enthuse about the non-locality of mind believe that by throwing in Fröhlich oscillators they can persuade mankind of the reality of non-locality of mind. However, to people like myself, who worked with Fröhlich and his oscillators, this seems more doubtful. Fröhlich dealt with solid state physics, and his oscillators (already known earlier in slightly different form in solid state physics) refer to matter and not to mind. It is therefore difficult to see an analogy between solid state systems and minds.

2.2 C.J.S. Clarke's Vista of Non-Locality

Chris Clarke is a Professor of Applied Mathematics at Southampton University. He published an interesting paper on non-locality of mind (Clarke, 1995) which one must, at least, read, even, if, like myself, one prefers a local theory of mentality. Interestingly Clarke, in passing, states near the start of his paper (op. cit. p. 231) that 'there is... a prevalence of authors arguing that mind is located in some higher dimensional space'

Let me state, therefore, at once, that my postulated Shadow Matter brain is as three-dimensional as the ordinary matter brain to which it is assumed to be (normally) attached. Likewise, my theory does not require that mental entities (such as qualia), where they have spatial properties at all, are more than three-dimensional. This, of course, is a matter of hypothesis, since we have no guarantee that things, like the objects around us, which appear to be three-dimensional, need to be three-dimensional. Appearances could be deceptive. However, the three-dimensionality of the perceived world is, probably, one of the simplest postulates to posit.

Clarke (1995, p. 331) is saying that mind 'is not located in space at all'. He goes even further and claims that mind 'is not located in ordinary 3-D physical space and that it is not located in a higher dimensional space, and it is not located *in* a generalized space'. In view of these drastic assumptions, which Clarke hurls at us, it would have been more satisfying if his paper contained a discussion of 'out-of-the-body-experiences'. In these the 'mind' (or mentality) seems to move with the 'apparent body' from the mind's original position in the normal body to the apparent 'out-of-the-body-position' of that body.

In this new position, the mind perceives the world just as it would if the normal body had been placed in the new position. This can be conveniently explained by assuming, as in Chapter 1, that normal 'mind' is fixed to and located at the locality

Consciousness & Near Death Experiences 53

of the Shadow Matter brain. During an OBE (= out of the body experience) the Shadow Matter body, and with it the Shadow Matter brain moves to the new out-of-the-body- position. And with the Shadow Matter brain moves the 'mind'.

However, one need not assume that 'the mind' is a spatial entity, as I have just done. One can simply embrace epiphenomenalism (cf. Wassermann 1979) and assume that there is no entity, called 'the mind'. Instead one can assume that there is only the Shadow Matter brain (which could be regarded as a modern version of a material soul). Certain changes of states of the Shadow Matter brain lead epiphenomenally to specific conscious experiences (e.g. qualia, concepts (i.e. meaning) etc.). Thus consciousness is not an entity but a property (namely a construct) of the Shadow Matter brain. In science one must distinguish between entities and properties of entities. When, during an OBE, the Shadow Matter brain shifts position, then its activation could still, as before, lead to epiphenomena and awareness of things, concepts etc. Thus I am not saying that 'mind' is located in an ordinary 3-D physical space, or in any other kind of space. I am simply denying that there is an object of any kind called 'the mind' which is attached to the body or to the Shadow Matter body (e.g. the Shadow Matter brain). Mentality in my theory is simply a consequence of activating the Shadow Matter brain, the activation producing consciousness, as epiphenomena of the induced activity of the Shadow Matter brain. But having stated my point of view so far, let me return to Clarke's (1995) paper.

Clarke (1995, p. 231) raises the possibility of an n-dimensional Euclidean space as the carrier of mind. He does this on the grounds that 'the many higher-dimensional physical theories that are in vogue all involve spaces that are *not* Euclidean'. While this gets rid of one kind of generalized spaces, one is still left with an entity called 'the mind', at least for those who wish to invoke such an entity, which I have thrown overboard above.

If one abandons the 'mind' as an entity but *not* as a generic term then one does not have to search, *via* sophisticated mathematics, what sort of space it resides in. But Clarke (rather than embrace epiphenomenalism, and with it materialism, possibly for religious or philosophical reasons) retains 'the mind' as a spatial entity.

Thus, I am not saying, like Clarke (1995, p. 331), that mind 'is not located in space at all'. I am denying that there is an entity called 'mind', and, hence, that no such entity can be located anywhere. For consciousness to be a byproduct of an active state of matter (say of the Shadow Matter brain) one does not need, as far as I can see, an extra entity called mind. The invoked byproducts, i.e. epiphenomena, suffice. This, of course, may not please religious people, but then I am a mechanistic materialist (see Wassermann, 1994). But I must deal further with Clarke's (mentalistic?) position, lest it is claimed that I have been unfair to him.

Next, Clarke throws out *curved space* as providing a home for mind. As he retains mind, the previous strictures still apply. Likewise metric spaces, topological spaces and fuzzy spaces are also not localities where mind is found.

The Shadow Matter brain is postulated (by me) to exist in a three-dimensional Euclidean space. So why does one have to bring in a mind, linked to it, in an esoteric kind of space, only to find, time and again, that this does not work? If many of the epiphenomena have also 3D structure in a 3D-Euclidean space, and if no mind is required, then, surely, the problems disappear.

Clarke (1995, p. 232) accepts Descartes' position that the *existence* of mind is axiomatic. This, of course, is to be expected if mind is dispensable, as argued, repeatedly, above. This prompts me even more to throw out the existence of mind as a useless and redundant axiom, which is not needed for any purposes of this book.

Nevertheless Clarke lingers. He states that 'it is logically inconsistent for *me* to postulate the non-existence of mind because without mind there is no me (see Cottingham, 1992).' A mechanistic materialist can, however, reject this Cartesian fallacy. If there is no *entity* called mind, but only epiphenomena of the activated Shadow Matter brain, then there can exist mentality *via* the epiphenomena but not *via* an entity called the mind. This, I believe, resolves the Cartesian fallacy that Clarke adopts.

2.3 Mind as a generic Term and some Remarks on Epiphenomenalism

If one maintains that mind is not an entity, but a generic term, then does this mean that one denies the existence of mentality? Not at all! According to epiphenomenalists mental experiences are byproducts (i.e. epiphenomena) of the activities of certain physical entities. But does a 'byproduct' of the activity of a physical thing not have to be itself a physical thing? Not necessarily! A byproduct of a thing need not necessarily resemble the thing of which it is a byproduct. Thus lemon juice is the byproduct of an object called a lemon. But the juice of a lemon, while resembling other lemon juice of the same lemon or of other lemons, does not resemble the lemon as a whole.

The question has often been asked (cf. Clarke, 1995) how are byproducts of matter (i.e. epiphenomena) produced? The fact that this question cannot be answered does not mean that epiphenomenalism as a *metaphysical* hypothesis is invalid. For all we know there may be an answer which evades us now or, perhaps, permanently. The type of epiphenomenalism which I envisage considers that the system which produces epiphenomena is not the ordinary matter brain. (This is widely, but, perhaps, wrongly assumed, cf. Wassermann (1993).) But it could be the Shadow Matter brain which, by hypothesis is bound to the ordinary matter brain. Thus, by metaphysical hypothesis activities of the Shadow Matter brain produce epiphenomena.

When, as my theory (Wassermann, 1993) assumes, in 'Out of the Body Experiences' the Shadow Matter brain becomes detached from the ordinary matter brain, then the Shadow Matter brain can still produce epiphenomena. But it is not the ordinary matter brain that produces the epiphenomena. Thus, what moves away from the ordinary matter body with the Shadow Matter brain to the locality taken up by the Shadow Matter brain, is the capacity of the Shadow Matter brain to make epiphenomena.

This explanation harmonizes with many of the facts of 'out of the body experiences'. The capacity to produce epiphenomena remains, according to this theory, *localized* in the Shadow Matter brain. Thus a thing called 'mind' may not exist and be neither localizes nor non-localized, the representatives of mentality, namely epiphenomena are produced in localities of the Shadow Matter brain.

There have been, and sure will be, various fallacious arguments which supposedly demolish epiphenomenalism. One such argument was manufactured by the late philosopher Sir Karl Popper. I refuted his argument in the journal *Mind* (Wassermann 1979). Popper based his alleged refutation on a supposed argument of the theory of evolution. Closer inspection shows that Popper's argument is invalid. I refer interested readers to my 1979 paper. I thought, however, that instead of just showing that Popper is wrong, as he was, it is preferable to develop a modern version of epiphenomenalism. I did this in a paper titled 'Materialism and Mentality' published in *Review Of Metaphysics* (1982) *35*, 715-729.

What is, perhaps astonishing is that Clarke (1995), in common with many other writers on that topic seems to disregard 'Out of the Body Experiences'. These have a central bearing (at least in my own work, cf. Wassermann (1993)) on the so-called 'Locality of Mind' and 'Non-locality of Mind' problems. But this is not the end of the story One also has to explain in connection with the mentality-localization problem where engrams are localized. In an earlier book (Wassermann, 1978) I dealt with the long-standing problem that engaged, for many years, the great neuropsychologist Karl Lashley, notably in his essay 'In Search of the Engram'. To Lashley, who, like Clarke, believed that mentality is located in the ordinary matter brain, the problem was to find where, precisely, engrams were located in the ordinary matter brain. Suppose, however, engrams are located in the Shadow Matter brain. In 'out of the body experiences' subjects remember what they experienced during the OBE. It seems plausible to assume that in an OBE the human memory, as well as the capacity to form new engrams, move with the Shadow Matter brain away from the ordinary matter brain. Likewise, it could be assumed that when the Shadow Matter brain is attached to the ordinary matter brain, then the engrams are located on the Shadow Matter brain and *not* on the ordinary matter brain. If so, then engrams are composed not of ordinary matter but of Shadow Matter. When an engram is activated, in this kind of model, then the activated engram could give rise to an epiphenomenon, which represents the *conscious* aspect of the engram.

2.4 The Case for localized mentality (including Consciousness.)

If mentality were not normally accurately localized in the head but, instead, spread from the head into the surrounding world, then this would raise some serious problematics. To start with we know that an accurately wired-in nervous system has evolved. In fact, that Cajal Class I neurons are very accurately wired-in is suggested by Palay's (1967) observations. Jacobson (1969, p. 543) remarked that in normal ontogeny:

> '. . . developing neurons sprout slender processes, their axons and

dendrites, which in some cases grow to relatively great lengths to form connections with other neurons. The direction of growth of these processes and the targets on which they terminate appear to be constant in all individuals of the same species. Anatomical and physiological methods have shown the remarkable invariance of neuronal circuits and have given no evidence of random connectivity. A distinguished neuroanatomist (Palay, 1967) has recently written, "the nervous system is not a random net. Its units are not redundant. Its organization is highly specific, not merely in terms of the connections between particular neurons, but also in terms of number, style, and location of terminals upon different parts of the same cell and the precise distribution of terminals arising from that cell."'

Even the most hard-nosed advocate of non-localized mentality (e.g. consciousness) will have to admit that the nervous system has something to do with mentality. That the nervous system is not discussed in Clarke's (1995) paper is surprising, although Clarke may have confined himself to mentality, which may not be practicable. Suppose that mentality is located—determined by the shadow matter brain. Suppose also that the shadow matter brain is developmentally determined by the ordinary matter brain, which is accurately wired-in, with utmost precision, as Palay's finding indicate. Then the *precise localization* of the various parts of the nervous system are *via* the Shadow Matter brain likely to produce a strict localization of mentality (including consciousness).

Admittedly, there are philosophers such as Hilary Putnam, who claim that meanings are normally not in the head (see Putnam, 1981 cited in Wassermann, 1994, p. 176). Such philosophers are simply ignoring the very likely intracranial representation of meaning-representing concepts. Or do they think that concept-representing structures reside normally outside the head?

I conclude that because of the accurate localization of the nervous system, and of the shadow matter brain, mentality is also strictly localized, normally within the head. However, according to my theory there exist two, normally mutually attached brains, namely the ordinary matter brain composed of neurons and glia (etc.) and the Shadow Matter brain. Also, according to my theory, it is the Shadow Matter brain, which is the 'seat' of mentality, and not the ordinary matter brain. I argued that during an 'out of the body experience' the Shadow Matter brain (or a part of it) becomes temporarily detached from the ordinary matter brain and carries with it, thus, much or all existing mentality. Accordingly in such circumstances thinking, feeling, remembering (etc.) can be performed by the Shadow Matter brain 'out of the body'.

A mental experience can be localized without some important component of it having localized contents. Thus, the smell of a rose the taste of a lemon, and so forth, have no locality per se. However accompanying, say, the taste of a lemon may be an awareness of the locality on the tongue where the lemon piece is being tasted, due to the taste locality receptors on the tongue. Yet, absence of perception of localization does not imply that mentality is non-localized. It only means that the epiphenomena of some physical aspect of mentality do not have 'localization parameters'.

More generally, certain experiences are simply non-spatial. But this does not mean that the physical, intracranial, representatives of these experiences are non-localized. It could mean that the content of the experience, which is experienced as non-spatial, is localized within the cranium. In physics, observed things or situations may be associated with 'observables' i.e. parameters that specify physical state variables. Likewise physical states of the Shadow Matter brain may be associated with specific Shadow Matter physical variables. Some of these are 'localization parameters' which when activated give rise to an experienced localization. In all this it is important to distinguish between experienced localization of something and the localization of the physical representation of that 'something' in, say the Shadow Matter brain.

2.5 Localization of Mentality versus Non-localization in Physics

In his important book *Incompleteness, Nonlocality and Realism: A Prolegomenon to the Philosophy of Quantum Mechanics* Redhead (1987) concluded in Chapter 8 (1.c. p.169)

'So there it is—some sort of action-at-a-distance or (conceptually distinct) non-separability seems built into any reasonable attempt to understand the quantum view of reality. As Popper has remarked our theories are

"nets designed by us to catch the world". We had better face up to the fact that quantum mechanics has landed some pretty queer fish.'

There is then action-at-a-distance of some sort in quantum physics, according to the most sophisticated philosophy of that subject. This does not imply that there must also be action-at-a-distance between mentality-representing entities in a philosophy of mentality. Undoubtedly, many parapsychologists favour this possibility. It could provide one possible mechanism for explaining telepathy and clairvoyance. Yet, if action-at-a-distance is based on an inverse square law, then this could lead to well-known difficulties (cf. Wassermann, 1993).

For this reason I postulated an alternative mechanism for telepathy (Wassermann, 1993). Perhaps one ought to be open-minded, since an action-at-a-distance need not be of the inverse square law kind. Even then there exist no convincing arguments that action-at-a-distance of any kind applies to mentality-representing entities.

Now let me turn to a different, but related, topic, namely the nature of a possible soul. Many philosophers, notably Descartes, have postulated an immaterial soul. Others, since antiquity, notably Philo, have advocated a *material soul*. According to my theory there may well exist a material soul. If so, then this material soul is being identified with the Shadow Matter brain. It is, thus, detachable from the ordinary matter brain in an out-of-the body experience, and, likewise, at death. Accordingly, at death the detached soul could survive indefinitely, although this is not logically or empirically necessary. Shadow Matter of the kind postulated here is assumed to be immensely light (at least the shadow matter of which the soul (and rest of the Shadow Matter body) is assumed to be composed). It is much lighter than any ordinary matter. In particular the density of Shadow Matter is supposed to be much less than the density (=mass per unit volume) of any known ordinary matter.

The soul and the Shadow Matter brain are here identified. According to my theory, the Shadow Matter brain (and *not* the ordinary matter brain) is the seat of mentality (e.g. consciousness). It follows that in this model the soul is the seat of mentality, as has been suggested by many thinkers since antiquity. What counts, however, here is that the *material* soul can become detached from the ordinary matter brain (e.g. at death and also during an 'out-of-the-body experience'). By contrast, it is far from obvious how an immaterial soul could become detached from the ordinary matter body. Detachment means the undoing of bonds. This, in turn, assumes that the soul is normally bonded to the ordinary matter brain, and, hence, must have physical properties, which does not apply to the immaterial soul. As regards the soul, the following short extracts from Clarke's (1995) paper might, perhaps, interest some readers.

Clarke (1995, p. 238) writes:

'In order to explain how this non-Newtonian view can shed light on the nature of mind it will be useful to refer to the 'hard problem' of Chalmers (1995): the problem of explaining why, apparently, brain processes give rise to an experience; why there is such a thing as the view from inside such processes (what it is like to experience them) as well as the scientific observation from outside. For the dualist there is no problem at this point, because the dualist can postulate a separate soul that observes the brain processes from the inside and thereby generates the experience. The problem for the dualist comes later, in making sense of a dual world.'

Although I have postulated a soul, namely a material soul (i.e. the Shadow Matter brain) it is far from obvious that this soul can observe the brain processes either from the inside or in any meaningful sense. Nor is it clear in what sense this 'observation process' generates an experience. Clarke may have some (possibly inapplicable) analogy in mind, but what I have just cited from him does not seem transparent to me. I conclude that although a material soul can make good sense within my model, within Clarke's discussion the way in which he invokes a soul is far from clear, at least to me.

If we ask ourselves whether the soul to which Clarke refers is a 'material soul' (as I assume) or an 'immaterial soul' then also the situation is obscure. I agree, however, with Clarke (1995, p. 238) when he states that 'with Chalmers (1995) he would hold that the basic experiential aspects of consciousness cannot be explained in terms of existing physical categories, but require the addition of a fundamentally new area of science, associated with but not reducible to existing physics, corresponding to experience.' This, however, is inherent in the

Consciousness & Near Death Experiences

epiphenomenalism discussed earlier. The epiphenomena in my theory are byproducts of activities of the Shadow Matter brain. Indeed epiphenomena are non-physical things that accompany physical activities of the Shadow Matter brain (or material soul) according to my point of view. This, of course, does not tell us what sorts of things epiphenomena are. I don't believe that any physical analogy would help to resolve this mystery. Let me try to be clear in this context.

In my type of model we are not dealing with a 'duality' but with a triplet of systems. First there is the ordinary matter brain. Normally (but not in most out-of-the-body- experiences or in death) there is physically bonded to the ordinary matter brain a second system, namely the Shadow Matter brain (i.e. material soul). When the ordinary matter brain becomes activated it can *physically* activate the Shadow Matter brain. This secondary activation, in turn, can produce a tertiary activation of the non-physical systems that produce epiphenomena, thus giving rise to epiphenomena.

At this stage we may be tempted to ask *how* are epiphenomena produced by the physical system which is the Shadow Matter brain. To this, possibly there may be no answer now or ever, since we are asking how a physical thing generates a non-physical one. I am far from certain, however, that this apparently unanswerable question can be brushed aside, simply by saying that the answer requires the addition of a fundamentally new area of science (e.g. shadow matter). Where I believe to have advanced on the traditional ways of dealing with these problems is—via the Shadow Matter brain—explaining out-of-the-body-experiences. Also possible survival of the Shadow Matter brain (but *not* of the ordinary matter brain) after death (see also Wassermann, 1993)). Whether we explain consciousness via epiphenomena or otherwise the difficulties raised in any attempt at reductionism seem currently insurmountable.

The conscious contents of epiphenomena (e.g. qualia such as the smell of a rose) need not have spatial properties. Epiphenomena *per se* in order to be linked to the Shadow Matter brain must have spatial properties.

2.6 The Shadow Matter Brain as a Property-Detector System

Perceptually or other cognitively generated properties of things can be of many different kinds. They could be an intracranial representation of an inspected cube or the taste of a chewed lemon or the smell of perfume and so forth indefinitely. The conscious intracranial representation of any property is here assumed to be produced by the Shadow Matter brain. When such a representation takes place then it activates parts, or the whole, of the Shadow Matter brain in specific ways. This activates specific property-detecting systems, and their spatially associated epiphenomena-generating systems, thereby generating conscious experiences of the appropriate set of epiphenomena. This kind of model differs drastically from that of Wassermann (1978). The representatives of perceivable items, as well as the representatives of concepts are rigorously localized in the Shadow Matter brain.

The representations, however, need not be unique. Instead there could be multiple representations of the same representable item, or of the same engram. This could explain Lashley's (1950) findings of the apparent multiple presence of the same engram within the cranium (see the long discussions in Wassermann, 1978). Engrams are, in this model, anchored to the Shadow Matter brain (i.e. they are parts of it). In cases where the Shadow Matter brain becomes detached from the ordinary matter brain (e.g. in out-of-the-body-experiences or at death) the engrams could move with the Shadow Matter brain. In case of death they could survive with the Shadow Matter brain (i.e. soul), and during detachment of the Shadow Matter barin additional new engrams could be formed by the Shadow Matter brain.

According to Wassermann (1993) the Shadow Matter brain is a highly elastic system. Hence if geometrical Gestalten, which are represented, say by engrams, in the Shadow Matter brain, experience strain, they can become deformed. In this way many of the Gestalt transformations studied by Köhler (1938, 1940) could come about in this elastic medium. Also, according to Wassermann (1993), and in agreement with various observations, the Shadow Matter brain is, apparently, also linked during life to the ordinary matter brain. It is linked by a thin, very elastic, cord, which I also assume is made of the same kind of Shadow Matter as the Shadow Matter brain and the rest of the Shadow Matter body. When the Shadow Matter brain separates from the ordinary matter brain, then the thin elastic cord extends. But this assures, except in death, that the Shadow Matter brain remains residually linked to the ordinary matter brain.

Subsequently the cord can contract again ensuring that the Shadow Matter brain reunites with the ordinary matter brain. The existence of the thin elastic cord has been reported by various people (cf. Wassermann, 1993 for sources). The apparent elasticity of the thin cord, together with the assumption that it consists of the same kind of Shadow Matter as the Shadow Matter brain (and body) suggests that the Shadow Matter brain (and body) are also highly elastic, in agreement with the preceding assumptions.

When the Shadow Matter brain separates from the ordinary matter brain and moves about in space, then the previous localities of the Shadow Matter brain that were associated with particular engrams remain associated with the engrams with which they were associated. It has also been reported by Blackmore (1993) that somebody had an 'out-of-the-body' experience as a result of riding a motorbike. This could be explained as follows in terms of the present theory. Riding a motorbike could set up relative vibratory motions between the Shadow Matter brain and the ordinary matter brain, leading to the separation of the bonds between the two brains, thus enabeling the Shadow Matter brain to move away from the ordinary matter brain and, likewise, the rest of the shadow matter body from the ordinary matter body. Yet in some, possibly many, cases of 'out-of-the-body' (=OBE) cases it is likely that only part of the Shadow Matter body, but not the whole of it becomes detached from the ordinary matter body. Otherwise, e.g. in the case of having an OBE while riding a motorbike it would be hard to see how the percipient of the OBE could still steer the motorbike on the assumption that perception and thinking (etc.) are controlled by the Shadow Matter brain. If I remember correctly, Dr. Celia Green wrote to me about a preacher who in his OBE watched himself from the back of a church giving a sermon in the front (see Blackmore 1993, p. 170). In order to control the motor systems of his body at least part of his Shadow Matter brain (according to the present theory) must have acted on his ordinary matter brain. If so, that part of the Shadow Matter brain could not have migrated with the rest to the back of the church. I have already discussed this likely 'splitting' of the Shadow Matter brain elsewhere (Wassermann 1993). Such 'split Shadow Matter brain' cases show that the problems and machinery of localization of the Shadow Matter brain and, with it, of mentality are very complex. However, from the case just cited it cannot be concluded that the Shadow Matter brain and mentality are not localized. It can only be concluded that occasionally, in abnormal circumstances, there occurs a splitting of the Shadow Matter brain followed by a separation of the split parts.

In one of the OBEs cited earlier (from Blackmore, 1993, pp. 164–167) there occurs the statement from the OBEr 'Then suddenly I was floating above my body linked to it by what appeared to be a shimmering cord'. Or in an OBE case history recorded by Celia Green (1976 p. 116) there occurs the statement already mentioned 'I seemed to be floating above myself rather like a balloon attached to a string, but I could not see how I was attached....' In these statements, and others, not cited here, there occurs clear reference to the thin cord mentioned earlier, which, by my hypothesis, links the Shadow Matter brain and the ordinary matter brain during separation. The thin cord must be highly elastic and very extensible, since, in the case just mentioned (and also earlier) the OBEr suddenly seemed to be 50–100 ft. above the OBEr's ordinary body, so that the cord would have extended between 50 and 100 ft. Yet, in all this, mentality is assumed to remain localized on the Shadow Matter brain, while the latter changes its position relative to the ordinary matter brain. Another, somewhat similar case, which I remember vividly, but of whose source I have lost sight of (but believe it comes from some publication by Celia Green) relates an OBE in which the OBEr located at the ground of a church tower suddenly experienced himself located high up at a gallery of the church tower. Here, again, the state of affairs resembles that of the preceding case.

I have already noted that, according to my theory, in an OBE the bonds linking the Shadow Matter brain and the ordinary matter brain snap. This breakage of bonds could conceivably be induced by chemical means. Significantly Blackmore (1993, p. 170) reports that:

> *'Some drugs are associated with OBEs; for example, the psychedelics— LSD, psilocybin and mescaline. More specific however, is the dissociative anaesthetic ketamine which often induces feelings of floating [typical of many OBEs] and even dying (Grinspoon & Bakalar, 1979; Rogo, 1984). I have had OBEs myself with this drug, though not as vivid as naturally occurring ones.'*

According to my theory (Wassermann, 1993) various altered states of consciousness could be induced by either weakening of the bonds or breaking of the bonds between the Shadow Matter brain and the ordinary matter brain. For instance, in an anaesthetic state such a weakening of many or all the bonds concerned could take place. Accordingly ketamine could be a bond-weakening and/or bond breaking chemical, which, in appropriate dosage could lead to bond breaking on a scale that leads to partial or complete dissociation between Shadow Matter brain and ordinary matter brain, resulting in an OBE. Similar remarks could apply to some of the other drugs mentioned above.

Blackmore (1993, p. 170) states that Celia Green describes one poor woman who seemed to be sitting [during an OBE] on the roof of her car the entire way through her driving test, unable to get back in and 'watching the body part of me making every sort of fool of myself that one could possibly manage in a limited time (Green, 1968 p. 64).'

Here again, one could assume a splitting of the Shadow Matter brain. One of its parts remains bound to the ordinary matter brain and, among other things, helps to control the motor system of the body that produces the steering and other driving control actions of the car. The other part of the assumed split Shadow Matter brain could then separate from the ordinary matter brain and move with the rest of the separated Shadow Matter body to the roof of the car. Each of the two separated parts of the Shadow Matter brain is assumed to be able to perform appropriate cognitive tasks.

I noted already in Section 1.1 that in many a typical near death experience (NDE) there occurs an OBE. This too could be due to a weakening and/or dissolution of bonds between the Shadow Matter brain and the ordinary matter brain. At death there could occur a complete dissociation between the two brains with all mutual bonds becoming dissociated. The detached Shadow Matter brain could then possibly survive in its completely detached state.

2.7 Localization within the Soul (= Shadow Matter brain)

In Wassermann (1993) I suggested that the Shadow Matter brain arises, during development of the ordinary matter brain. The ordinary matter brain could serve for the genesis of the Shadow Matter brain much as a photographic negative can serve as the generator of a 'positive' photo. In (W93) I made this notion more detailed. I assumed that to every ordinary matter electron there corresponds, in the Shadow Matter world, a Shadow Matter electron (called selectron).

Yet, it would be quite mistaken, as a confused reader of Wassermann (1993) did, to assume that a selectron is an exact duplicate of an electron. To start with, the selectron, unlike the electron, consists of shadow matter, and not of ordinary matter, and shadow matter differs from ordinary matter (see Kolb, *et al.* 1985). Moreover, if an electron should not be a point particle but have an 'internal structure' *and if the same should apply to the selectron*, then the internal structure of the selectron could differ from the internal structure of the electron. I conclude that the relation between electron and selectron could in some crude way resembles the relation between a photographic negative and a photographic positive. Yet an electron and a selectron need in no way be similar, let alone be exact duplicates.

Similar remarks apply to other elementary particles of ordinary matter and their Shadow Matter correspondents. Thus, to an ordinary matter quark (say an upquark) there corresponds an appropriate Shadow Matter quark (=squark). Again the squark need in no way be similar to the quark to which it corresponds, let alone be an exact duplicate of the latter. Also consider the building up of ordinary matter out of electrons and quarks (via forming atomic nuclei out of quarks and gluons and by forming atoms out of atomic nuclei and electrons). Something corresponding (but not exactly duplicating) could happen in the Shadow Matter world. To a specific kind of ordinary matter atom (say a sodium atom) there could correspond, in the world of shadow matter, a specific kind of shadow matter atom (=satom). (Say, in the example given a sodium satom made up of a snucleus and selectrons). Again, it must be stressed that a sodium satom is not a duplicate, let alone an exact duplicate, of a sodium atom. Similarly to each different kind of atom there corresponds a specific type of satom. (To give another example, to a hydrogen atom there corresponds a hydrogen satom.) Similar remarks apply to the Shadow Matter analogues of ordinary matter molecules. To a particular molecule there corresponds a particular kind of smolecule in the Shadow Matter world. The smolecule which corresponds to the molecule is assumed to be built up of satoms such that to each atom (or ion) of the molecule there corresponds a satom (or sion) of the smolecule. Thus, to the water molecule H_2O there corresponds the smolecule sH_2sO and to the sulphuric acid molecule H_2SO_4 there corresponds the smolecule sH_2sSsO_4, and so forth.

One of the principal assumptions is that corresponding atoms and satoms of the same name match each other (and likewise an electron matches a selectron and a quark matches a squark of the same name). Matching atom and satom can become bound to each other, because they are assumed to be complementary in structure. It must be stressed again that an atom and satom of the same name (except for the attached s of the satom) are not exact duplicates of each other although they are assumed to be structurally complimentary. Thus, for example, a hydrogen atom H can become bound to a sH satom, the bond being a bond between ordinary matter and shadow matter. Likewise it is assumed that a molecule can bind a smolecule of the same name, so that, for example H_2O can bind sH_2sO.

The present theory assumes that the human Shadow Matter body is bound to the human ordinary matter body with each satom of the former being bound to a corresponding atom of the latter. Similarly to each smolecule of the human Shadow Matter body there corresponds a molecule of the human ordinary matter body. To atoms, which bind other atoms there, correspond similarly named (but not exact duplicate) satoms that bind other satoms, and so forth. In this fashion the atoms of the ordinary matter brain bind satoms of the Shadow Matter brain, and in this way the ordinary matter brain binds the Shadow Matter brain. More generally, in this way, the ordinary matter body binds the Shadow Matter body.

In an out-of-the body experience (OBE) part or the whole of the Shadow Matter body separates from part or the whole of the ordinary matter body. Typically in an OBE part or whole of the Shadow Matter brain can become detached from the ordinary matter brain according to this theory. Also not every Shadow Matter satom can become bound to every other ordinary matter atom. Only a satom of the same name as an atom can become bound to that atom, and similar remarks apply to smolecules and molecules.

Conditions which favour detachement of the Shadow Matter brain from its attachement to the ordinary matter brain are any conditions that favour breakage of bonds between shadow matter and ordinary matter. The notion that Shadow Matter can become bound to ordinary matter is an intrinsic aspect of the present theory. In the realm of ordinary matter there exists complementarity between, say, an enzyme (macro) molecule and the substrate molecule on which it acts. Likewise it is assumed that there exists complementarity between any atom and the satom which it can bind and also between any molecule and the smolecule which it can bind. Complementarity is something vaguely analogous to the structural matching of a photo and its negative.

The postulated human material soul (= Shadow Matter brain) has localities within it minutely specified by the localization of its component satoms and the component smolecules which are composed of satoms. The present model of the Shadow Matter brain and its relation to the ordinary matter brain, notably its reversible detachability from the latter, is based on a minute localization of satoms etc. within the *material soul*, i.e. Shadow Matter brain. According to this the soul is composed of matter, namely Shadow Matter.

Also according to this model it is not the ordinary matter brain that is conscious, but the Shadow Matter brain, when activated. Moreover conscious experiences, which are here identified with epiphenomena, are assumed to be localized by strict location of the epiphenomena at precise loci of the Shadow Matter brain (or soul). In this fashion each satom of the soul could locate a very specific item of consciousness. The various items of consciousness could form a whole, resembling, perhaps vaguely, the psychic aspect of Wolfgang Köhler's (1938, 1940) psychophysical isomorphism. In the present theory mentality, in the form of epiphenomena produced by the Shadow Matter brain (or soul), is localized in the soul.

This point of view differs drastically from that of C.J.S. Clarke (1995) who advocated a 'nonlocality of mind'. One major aspect of the present model is the detachability of the Shadow Matter brain (or soul) from the ordinary matter brain in an OBE. As far as I can see there is no explanation of OBEs of the kind given here and in Wassermann (1993) in Clarke's (1995) paper. In fact, there is no discussion of OBEs in Clarke's paper. If he has heard of OBEs and simply disregarded them, then this is, in my opinion, a serious omission. Indeed, without discussing OBEs thoroughly there is no justification to jump to the conclusion, reached by Clarke, that mentality is nonlocalized. In fact, OBEs are a thorn in the flesh of many, possibly most, anti-parapsychologists (i.e. people who do not believe in the genuineness of psychic phenomena). Not very long ago somebody I have known for many years insisted that OBEs do not exist. When I told him that he is silly he broke off our long-standing friendship.

When, in an OBE a part, or the whole, of the soul becomes detached from the ordinary matter brain, then mentality continues to reside in the Shadow Matter brain (or soul) and moves with it away from the ordinary matter brain. When reattachment of soul and ordinary matter brain occur, then mentality, via the soul, will again be located as it was before separation of the soul and the ordinary matter brain. Also at death there occurs, in my model, not only clinical death of the kind that can be medically detected by familiar means. But the Shadow Matter body becomes *completely* detached from the ordinary matter body.

It remains then possible that, just as in an OBE, the Shadow Matter brain that becomes detached retains its capacity to form conscious experiences via giving rise to epiphenomena. The Shadow Matter brain, i.e. the soul, also retains the engrams which, according to this theory, it localized during life. Thus, the age-old notion of body and soul recurs here.

The soul is now identified with the Shadow Matter brain. More generally there exists (according to Wassermann, 1993) a Shadow Matter body of which the Shadow Matter brain, i.e. soul, forms only a part. The part of the Shadow Matter body which does not belong to the Shadow Matter brain, is normally assumed to be bound to the rest of the ordinary matter body, i.e. to that part of the ordinary matter body which is not bound to the Shadow Matter brain. In an OBE it is quite possible that in some, or many, cases much or almost all of the Shadow Matter body becomes also detached from the ordinary matter body and remains coherent with the Shadow Matter brain. At death the whole of the Shadow Matter body, including the Shadow Matter brain, is assumed to move away from the ordinary matter body or what remains of it.

The present theory, while involving a dualism of ordinary matter body and Shadow Matter body, is not a Cartesian kind of dualism. Descartes envisaged a *non*-material soul, whereas the present theory postulates a material soul (i.e. the postulated Shadow Matter brain). The Shadow Matter body (including its Shadow Matter brain) does not resemble the ordinary matter body. It is not an exact duplicate of the latter or, for that matter, any kind of duplicate, it follows that if there is any survival of the detached Shadow Matter body after death that the surviving Shadow Matter body need not resemble the previously existing ordinary matter body.

This raises serious problems for spiritualists. (Let me stress, at once, that I am a mechanistic materialist (see Wassermann 1994) and not a spiritualist.) Although my model makes a surviving Shadow Matter body a strong possibility, it makes any resemblance of that shadow matter body and the body which it inhabited before death, very unlikely. Hence, if trance mediums state that they can see the 'spirits' of the dead, and that these spirits resemble the previously living bodies, that they carry 'flowers' etc., then this seems very unconvincing. Even should these mediums see the surviving Shadow Matter body of the dead, then it is far from clear how they could recognize the surviving shadow matter body as having belonged to the dead body.

If it seems unlikely that living people can visually perceive the surviving Shadow Matter bodies of dead persons, then this does not necessarily exclude communication between living people and surviving souls of dead people. Perhaps the simplest way to explain this is by assuming that telepathy (as interpreted in Wassermann (1993) in terms of Shadow Matter theory) takes place between a surviving soul and the soul of a living person, say a trance medium. Thus telepathy need not only take place between the souls (i.e. Shadow Matter brains) of two living people, but it could take place between the surviving soul of a dead person and the soul of a living person. Telepathy could also take place between the soul of one surviving person and the soul of another surviving person. Also a more familiar possibility is that telepathy occurs between the soul of one living person and the soul of another living person. I shall return to the possible mechanism of telepathy later in this book.

In order that people can understand each other in ordinary discourse, they require, according to the present theory, corresponding souls which are endowed with corresponding Shadow Matter machinery. In everyday perception of speech, I assume that within the Shadow Matter brain of the speaker the speech act is produced in Shadow Matter code. This, then, activates via the ordinary matter brain the speech machinery of the speaker. The, thus, produced speech activates the ordinary matter brain of the listener and, via this, activates the Shadow Matter brain (= soul) of the listener, leading, via epiphenomena to the conscious perception of the speech received.

2.8 Genetic Determination of Localization within the Soul

Many localities within the soul, and their Shadow Matter components, and the specificities of the latter are likely to be innate and, thus, genetically determined. Genes are most unlikely to act directly on the soul, but could do so, indirectly, via the ordinary matter brain, which, itself, is genetically determined. Genes can be expected to act during development of the ordinary matter body and its ordinary matter brain. During this genetic fashioning of the ordinary matter body in various phases of development one could expect that newly arising parts of the ordinary matter body (and brain) give rise to newly generated parts of the Shadow Matter body and its soul. In this way genes can, via the ordinary matter body development, control the development of the Shadow Matter body, including its soul.

As the genes belong to the ordinary matter body they can no longer influence the Shadow Matter body (including the soul) after death. This means that the soul is genetically controlled during lifetime (namely indirectly). Such genetic control of the soul ceases at death, so that all that the soul ever inherits from ancestors via genes will have been inherited before death.

Perhaps something should also be said about how the soul acquires the energy for its transactions. Otherwise it might be suspected that energy is not being conserved and, hence, the first law of thermodynamics might seem to be infringed. However, the driving energizing system of the soul is the ordinary matter brain and its metabolism. At least this is assumed to apply while the ordinary matter brain and the soul remains linked. But what happens when the soul (i.e. the Shadow Matter brain) becomes detached from the ordinary matter brain? It may be assumed that during OBEs and after death the soul persists on previously stored energy that it derived from the ordinary matter brain by energy transfer during life. This however could mean that the soul could only remain active, after death, until its stored, and required, energy is used up, after which death of the soul could occur. There exists, however, another possibility which I shall discuss in Chapter 3 (see Section 3.1).

According to this there could exist two kinds of Shadow Matter. One of these is the one discussed so far, which forms Shadow Matter bodies and their souls. This kind of Shadow Matter is assumed to be immensely light. In addition I shall assume that there exists a heavier type of Shadow Matter which surrounds the Earth surface like a coat. This heavier Shadow Matter could derive its energy from sunlight (via sphotons (= Shadow Matter photons). It could pass some of its energy gain to the 'dead' souls, thus prolonging their persistence in active states for an indefinite period, possibly millions of years. When ultimately the sun expands and engulfs the Earth I would not venture to predict what is likely to happen to surviving souls.

2.9 The Nonlocality of secondary encoded Mentality

Primary mentality is assumed to be encoded in the Shadow Matter brain (i.e. soul) and is localized within the soul. But in communication between the souls of two different people by means of telepathy the carriers of information that are involved in the communication are nonlocalized. These carriers are secondary encoders of mentality.

At this stage I must explain and stress that the notion of localization of both matter and mind is a difficult one. Let us consider a hydrogen atom. The quarks of its nucleus, while localized within the nucleus are not rigidly fixed in position. In fact they may be expected to change positions relative to each other within the nucleus. This, in fact, is what we might expect on the basis of quantum mechanics with its statistical interpretation of the position of point particles. This, of course, is on the assumption that quarks are point particles. If, as some theoreticians have argued quarks are not point particles but extended structures called superstrings (Green, 1985) then the notion of localization of a quark within a nucleus may be an even more difficult concept.

Likewise, when we consider the electron of a hydrogen atom then this poses similar localization problems. If the electron should be a point particle, then its localization within the atom is, again, statistically determined via quantum mechanics. If, on the other hand, the electron is a superstring, then the notion of its localization could pose difficulties. Even more complex localization problems arise for more complex multi-electron atoms. The complexity increases vastly more when we consider structural localization within molecules. An even very much more complex situation arises for macromolecules such as proteins, DNA and RNA and their complexly folded structures where, and if, present.

The localization issues become even vastly more intricate when we come to animal or plant cells and whole organisms or organs. Localization of cells (etc.) within a brain exhibits the problematic at its most obvious.

My model of the soul (= Shadow Matter brain) postulates, to each ordinary matter atom there is attached a correspondingly named satom (which, by assumption differs from the atom). The localization of each satom of the soul corresponds to the localization of the atom of the brain to which it is attached by

Consciousness & Near Death Experiences

means of appropriate atom-satom bonds. Thus, as regards localization, but not composition and structure, the soul and the ordinary matter brain resemble each other. The different composition and structure of the soul and the ordinary matter brain could be related to the reason why the soul is the seat of consciousness and mentality. The ordinary matter brain, by contrast, could just be an intermediate channeling system that has evolved as a mediator between the external world (via various other nervous system components) and the soul.

During an OBE, the soul separates from the ordinary matter brain (or a part of the soul separates from a part of the ordinary matter brain). Then the relative localization of components of the soul is assumed to remain as it was while soul and body were united. It must also be stressed that according to my theory (Wassermann, 1993) the Shadow Matter brain (= soul) can pass through ordinary matter bodies of all kinds, except the ordinary matter brain to which it can bind. More generally, this applies to all kinds of other Shadow Matter bodies, which can penetrate through all kinds of ordinary matter bodies, except ordinary matter bodies to which they can bind. Similarly, it could be expected that ordinary matter bodies can pass, without resistance, through Shadow Matter bodies of a kind to which they cannot bind. These remarks, let me stress, do not only apply to living bodies and to Shadow Matter related to living matter. They apply also to inanimate matter and Shadow Matter related to inanimate (and animate) matter. Thus, the world of ordinary matter can be passed through by the world of souls and *vice versa* (apart from exceptions mentioned).

Perhaps something more ought to be said at this stage about the *Problems of Personal Identity* as related to organisms that are by assumption composed both of ordinary matter and Shadow Matter.

2.10 Aspects of Personal Identity

I shall first cite a modified passage from Wassermann (1994, p. 231–232). There I wrote:

> *Organisms, such as amoebae, let alone human beings, cannot profitably be described in terms of sufficiently complex quantum chemistry. Some of their chemical subcomponents can be described in such terms. Nevertheless, for some complex systems, surprisingly perhaps, including*

human beings, one can suggest in terms of SYMOs (= Systemic Models) what is the 'It that remains the same while the attributes of the thing change' (a question posed by Nussbaum and based on Aristotle). For humans and all other organisms one makes the biological distinction between phenotype (which represents the observable traits, including behavioural traits) of an organism and its genotype. (The genotype lists the genes that an organism contains) (stating the alleles of these genes present) and the location and mode of relative arrangements of these genes within 'genomes' i.e. gene carrying systems). There exists no easily demonstrable connection between phenotype and genotype. It is possible to suggest, via SYMOs, how during normal development the genotype determines systematically the phenotype (cf. Wassermann, 1972, now dated or better Clowes and Wassermann, 1984). Accordingly one could answer the Aristotelian question of Nussbaum by asserting that the genotype of an organism, is the principal invariant that remains unchanged. The phenotype may change in numerous ways. Moreover, if the organism, after change, is restored to its former state, then it is a consequence of its genotype that it favours certain 'steady states'.

The philosopher Ardon J. Lyon asks in *An Encyclopaedia of Philosophy* (G.H.R. Parkinson ed., Routledge 1988) p. 441: 'What is it to remain one and the same person over a period of time?' No simple answer can be given. One of the answers that can be given is that (see above) our genotype remains unaltered. But certainly not our phenotype. For instance, we acquire new memories much of the time and in this sense do not remain the same person. So, perhaps, while we do not really remain the same person for any length of time, some aspects of our personality, namely our genotype remains the same. Since our phenotype (e.g. our outward appearance) is only very complexly related to our genotype, there is no easy way of claiming that personal identity is represented by our phenotype. Important aspects of this identity may, throughout life, be represented by our genotype. Lyon (p. 441), instead of fastening on genes (or genotypes) as the nonchanging elements of the body (although genes can be in active or inactive states) asks 'Does this mean that there is something that *doesn't* change while body, characters and memories alter, something we might call the soul, and that

Consciousness & Near Death Experiences

that is what the person essentially is?'

In the previous sections I identified the soul with the Shadow Matter brain, and according to the present theory the Shadow Matter brain is the seat of memories and other important systems that change throughout life. Again Lyon writes that 'If we are immaterial souls, then perhaps we might survive our bodily death.' *Pace* Lyon's conclusions, I have argued that our soul is material and consists of Shadow Matter. Even such a material soul, by becoming detached from the material body at death could survive (see above).

Beside this Lyon suggests that we lack a clear idea of what a soul is. In contrast to this I have argued at length, earlier on, that a soul can be carefully defined in terms of a Shadow Matter system. I have argued *that* and *how* a material soul could exist, notwithstanding Lyon's doubts on that topic. Also the material soul is assumed to be invisible (just as Plato envisaged for the immaterial soul, which is here rejected).

Lyon (1988, p. 442) points out that the philosopher John Locke 'was indeed one of the first philosophers to discuss the question of personal identity in sophisticated detail. He argued that to remain the same soul, to remain the same person, and to remain the same man (or woman) were three quite different things. A soul, a person and a man are three different things.' If, however, we rely on a material soul, namely a Shadow Matter brain, then this is unlikely to remain the same throughout much or most of life. Since the soul forms an essential component of a person (by hypothesis) we may also assume that a person alters throughout life, at least part of a person (but not its genotype).

When Lyon asks (l.c. p. 444) 'So what is it that provides the continuity between the present me and my past self?' then there can be several answers. First, as argued earlier, our genotypes provide one important, persisting element of continuity. Then there are such things as stored memories (i.e. engrams). Our genes are coded for by DNA and, via this, for messenger RNA and, hence for polypeptide chains of proteins. The proteins provide all kinds of structures and carry out all kinds of functions. None of these answers could have been given in Locke's time. Lyon (1988, p. 445) also claims that 'reincarnation does not as a matter of fact occur'. Who whispered this into Lyon's ear I do not know.

I have discussed the topic with Professor Ian Stevenson (US) who is one of the world's leading experts on the subject of reincarnation and has plenty of evidence that it occurs. (Ian Stevenson, M.D. is Carlson Professor of Psychiatry Box 152, University of Virginia Health Science Centre, Charlottesville, Virginia 22908 USA) and I shall discuss some of his important work in chapter 5 of this book. To argue as dogmatically as Lyon does strikes me as absurd and totally mistaken, based on ignorance. I do not think that Lyon has read any of Professor Stevenson's books on the subject. But Lyon remains a friend of mine.

According to my theory the soul or Shadow Matter brain provides another aspect of personal identity. As I have proposed (see also Wassermann, 1993) in an OBE the soul becomes partly or entirely detached from the ordinary matter brain. According to my theory the personal identity remains seated in the soul and moves with the soul. Likewise at death the soul would get completely detached from the ordinary matter brain and could survive. With it could survive the personal identity awareness of the soul's former owner (and the soul could develop further after death, e.g. form new engrams telepathically). Thus the ancient notion of a soul as a carrier of personal identity and the localization of the soul as well as the transmigration (or reincarnation) of the soul (see chapter 5) comes here again into its own in a somewhat more modern guise. The soul is here identified as a part of the Shadow Matter body. Perhaps I come here to conclusions not unlike those of Chalmers (1995) and C.J.S. Clarke (1995), discussed in a different context by Clarke (l.c. p. 238). Clarke writes:

> 'With Chalmers, I would hold that the basic experiential aspects of consciousness cannot be explained in terms of existing physical categories, but require the addition of a fundamentally new area of science, associated with but not reducible to existing physics, corresponding to experience.'

Indeed, in my own theory I have relied on the new science of Shadow Matter, which is autonomous. It cannot be explained in terms of existing physical categories, but it could explain paranormal phenomena (see Wassermann, 1988, 1993 and parts of this book). In this new theory experiential aspects of consciousness are localized in the Shadow Matter brain, i.e. the material soul. Conscious experiences *per se* while located in the soul are not material entities, but conscious phenomena are produced by the material soul as epiphenomena. Thus, according to this theory, the seat of production of epiphenomena is the material soul. This, however, does not explain how the soul produces epiphenomena, i.e. there is no known mechanism by which the soul produces epiphenomena.

Indeed, if epiphenomena are non-material one could hardly expect that a material soul explains how non-material epiphenomena arise. Although the hypothesis of the soul (= Shadow Matter brain) explains various aspects of OBEs. It also suggests the likely seat of consciousness. Yet it does not explain how the putative seat of consciousness (i.e. the soul) produces consciousness. The ultimate problem is that the ordinary matter brain and the material soul are something material. It is not clear how material systems can generate something non-material such as consciousness. One is dealing here with different kinds of entities, namely material ones and non-material ones. These are not problems of localization of material and non-material entities, but questions of *relationships* of entities of different kinds.

We can, of course, argue that in the world of matter (including, perhaps, the world of Shadow Matter) totally different kinds of matter can interact. Thus, in a macromolecule, such as a protein, many different amino acid molecules can become linked to form a polypeptide chain. Similarly, it is conceivable that, say, Shadow Matter can interact with non-matter (to which consciousness belongs). The mode of interaction might not be based on any kind of interaction between matter and matter. Thus the non-material carrier of consciousness could interact with appropriate categories of matter by (non-matter) interactions.

What such interactions are like, if they exist, is totally unknown. Unlike Descartes' non-material soul, the present material soul is definitely a member of the category of matter. The problem is how the non-matter consciousness entities interact with the material soul. Former thinkers have sometimes argued as if consciousness entities are components of the brain (e.g. in the mind/brain identity theories). The latter kind of materialism differs from the present type of materialism in which the material soul *per se* is not conscious but interacts with non-material consciousness entities. Whereas for Descartes the soul was non-material and interacted with the material ordinary matter brain, in the present model the soul is material and interacts with the ordinary matter brain and *also* interacts with consciousness entities. Thus the material soul has here two kinds of interactions. Thus, Descartes interaction dualism is here replaced by three interacting systems, namely the ordinary matter brain, the material soul and the consciousness entities.

What ordinary matter is like, we all know. What Shadow Matter could be like we know from Kolb *et al.*'s (1985) paper. Consciousness entities could consist of such things as qualia and other entities that express or convey consciousness. My model differs drastically in outlook from the point of view of Nobel Laureate Francis Crick of the Salk Institute. Crick asserts (according to the *Sunday Times Magazine* 1 December 1996, p. 55) 'that consciousness is the effect of brain cells oscillating globally across the neocortex at the rate of 40 hertz—that is 40 cycles per second.' It is totally obscure how Crick's proclamation could explain consciousness in OBEs. Possibly he denies OBEs. This is not unusual for people who find well established OBEs hard to explain. I know one such person, who denies the existence of OBEs and who refuses to have anything to do with me because I believe in them and have told him that his denials are absurd.

The Sunday Times continues:

> '*[Crick] 'bases his assertion on research that focuses on an enigma in brain science known as the 'binding problem': how do all the myriad impressions invading our nervous system become transformed into a single object of conscious attention? Or, put it another way, how do all the segregated mappings in the brain relating to size, distance, colour, shape, sound, direction, and so on, unify into a single object at a moment of what philosophers call 'intentionality'—for example, when a cat's attention is seized by a mouse. Scientists have observed the 40 hertz phenomenon in their experiments and have deduced that it is the best candidate for the 'binding' principle.'*

Contrary to this extract from the *Sunday Times Magazine*, one also has to explain many Gestalt phenomena (Köhler, 1938, 1940) in terms of a suitable brain model. This is not just a matter of explaining the binding problem. Then, as mentioned, one has to explain OBEs, which my kind of theory does explain (in terms of the Shadow Matter brain = soul). The same *Sunday Times Magazine* article (l.c. p. 56) also cites the Reverend Don Cupitt, 'famous for his belief in a materialist religion informed by the latest neuroscience and artificial intelligence work.'

'Consciousness', he says, 'is just electronic waves of excitation. What we are used to calling the mind or the soul is entirely on the surface of our heads and bodies—understanding finds its origins in the motor nerves that give rise to language and speech and a sort of fluttering that occurs in the soft palate and ends up in the ear.'

This again seems hard to reconcile with OBEs, and Cuppitt's view of the soul differs drastically from that espoused in the present book, where the soul is interpreted as a materialistic Shadow Matter brain. The possibility that in an OBE a Shadow Matter brain (or soul) may not be on the surface of our heads or bodies (cf. Wassermann, 1993) does not seem to enter Cupitt's natural philosophy. Cupitt is further quoted as saying that:

'When asked what his version of consciousness meant for Christianity, he confirmed that he had no faith in the survival of the soul beyond death: We have to learn to accept our own temporality, our own mortality, our finitude. The days are gone when we believed in the soul and free will, that the inner life is of supreme importance. The soul, the self, has died. The self is an animal with cultural inscriptions on its surface.'

Now most, or all, of this latter statement by Cupitt is repudiated in this book. The existence of a material soul, in the guise of a materialistic Shadow Matter brain is here affirmed. Moreover, as my interpretation of OBEs suggests, the soul can become detached from the ordinary matter brain and float off into space some distance away from the ordinary matter body. It can remain attached to the latter by the thin elastic cord discussed earlier. Also, at death a permanent detachment of the soul from the ordinary matter body could occur with the thin cord breaking. This could be accompanied by lengthy or even permanent survival of the soul, while the ordinary matter body disintegrates or undergoes some other form of decay. If, and when, the soul (= Shadow Matter brain) survives then the postulated, materialistic, consciousness entities could survive with the soul and attached to it.

In concluding this chapter I must briefly discuss the so-called 'hard problem' of consciousness a term used by Chalmers. On the one hand consciousness is an individual, if you like 'private', experience. On the other hand one can try to explain consciousness (or rather consciousness carriers) in terms of consciousness entities, as I have done above. The hard problem of consciousness is the problem how to unify a materialistic explanation of consciousness in terms of, say, consciousness entities and the private experience of consciousness.

In common with various other scientists and philosophers I doubt whether the hard problem has a solution. It seems that all past and present attempts to unify the nature of privately experienced consciousness with any proposed materialistic basis of consciousness has been and is unsuccessful. In order to reduce scientific entities, such as molecules, to atoms (and these to electrons and nuclei) one requires similarities of kinds. (Thus atomic nuclei are made up of quarks and gluon fields. Quarks are elementary particles (or possibly superstrings; cf. Green 1985), and electrons are also elementary particles (or possibly superstrings). The similarities of kinds in this case are that at the reductively lowest known levels at present in physics one is dealing with fundamental particles and interaction mediating fields. Typically gluon fields, electromagnetic (photon-mediated) fields etc. Unlike this, private experiences and possible material carriers of private experiences such as 'consciousness entities' are dissimilar in type, which seems to rule out reduction.

3. Possible Mechanisms Of The Near Death Experience (NDE)

3.1 The possible Machinery of Out-of-the-Body Experiences (OBEs)

A part of the present theory of OBEs is the same as that presented in Wassermann (1993). It is assumed that all ordinary material objects consist of atoms or ions. These in turn can, in many cases, form, by mutual bonding, molecules. Some of these can form macromolecules etc. A typical atom consists of a nucleus which is surrounded by an atom-specific number of electrons. These move round the nucleus. An atom's nucleus consists of a nucleus-specific number of up-quarks and down-quarks which are kept together within the nucleus by particles called gluons (via gluon fields).

According to my Shadow Matter theory (inspired by Kolb *et al.* (1985) and published in Wassermann (1993)) every quark can bind a corresponding Shadow Matter quark (called a squark for short). Thus an up-quark can bind a Shadow Matter up-quark. It is also assumed that every electron can bind a Shadow Matter electron called a selectron for short.

In this way every atom, made up of quarks and electron(s) can bind a Shadow Matter atom, called a satom for short. This is composed of selectron(s) and squarks. In addition to being bonded to quarks and electrons, respectively, squarks and selectrons could also interact by Shadow Matter-specific forces. Again, molecules can bind Shadow Matter molecules, called smolecules for short, and so forth for other types of ordinary matter. In this way all ordinary matter could bind specific (but not duplicate) types of Shadow Matter. For instance, a human body could bind a Shadow Matter body, and the brain could bind a Shadow Matter brain.

Unlike ordinary matter the postulated Shadow Matter which can bind to ordinary matter is assumed to be very light and very much lighter than ordinary matter. I shall call this light Shadow Matter or L-SM for short. This Shadow Matter was already postulated in Wassermann (1993). For instance, a selectron is very much lighter than an electron and a Shadow Matter up-quark is assumed to be much lighter than an ordinary matter up-quark.

In addition to this L-SM of my earlier theory, the present theory postulates that there exists a Shadow Matter which is heavier than L-SM and which is called Heavy Shadow Matter or H-SM for short and which is here identified with the SM of Kolb et al (1985) and which may be what astrophysicists call 'dark matter'. H-SM was not postulated in Wassermann (1993). L-SM and H-SM can also interact by Shadow Matter forces. In addition, as in Kolb *et al.* (1985), it is assumed that L-SM and ordinary matter can interact gravitationally.

In an OBE it is assumed that gravitational bonds between an ordinary matter human body (or parts of such a body) and the L-SM body (or parts of the L-SM body) which it binds become broken or 'snap'. The L-SM body and the ordinary matter body can then move apart. When this happens the H-SM, *which is supposed to surround the earth surface as an approximate spherical shell resembling a* H-SM *'ocean'*, can then act on the liberated L-SM body (or body part). Since the L-SM is, by assumption, much lighter than the H-SM, the H-SM can exert an upthrust on the freed part of the L-SM, which could then float upwards.

This could explain the *floating upwards* reported by many OBE percipients and noted in various cases of OBEs. The upward floating of the L-SM body could then continue until the light thin elastic cord (assumed to be made of Shadow Matter and discussed earlier) becomes tight. This links the L-SM body to the ordinary matter body to which it was originally bound L-SM, becomes so tight that it balances the upthrust on the body. My preceding explanation of the upward floating of the L-SM body resembles some aspects of Archimedes' principle in fluid mechanics. After death the elastic cord could become disconnected from the ordinary matter body, thus allowing further upward floating of the shadow matter body to 'heaven' near the top of the H-SM ocean.

To Blackmore, who is not a professional physicist this *type* of theory may seem 'ridiculous' (see Blackmore 1993 p. 139). Yet it is perfectly feasible in Kolb *et al*'s world of Shadow Matter physics, as presented in the journal *Nature*.

There are those who believe that OBEs are no more than hallucinations. Such a kind of explanation, however, gets nowhere. It does not explain why percipients of OBEs should hallucinate precisely the class characteristics of OBEs and not hallucinate quite different experiences. Why, for instance, should so many percipients just experience that they see their ordinary matter body from the outside and that they are floating upwards?

Earlier I stated that it is assumed that in an OBE the gravitational bonds between an ordinary matter human body and the L-SM body which it binds become broken or 'snap'. This snapping could explain the 'uncomfortable noise, a loud ringing or buzzing' which is often present in a NDE. The effect of the snapping of the bonds could be propagated via the Shadow Matter body to the 'sound representing' regions of the Shadow Matter brain. There it triggers the physical basis of the effects whose epiphenomena are the perceived buzzing.

3.2 Explaining the Tunnel Experience (TE)

Earlier I cited within the passage quoted from Moody that in a Near Death Experience (NDE) the experiencer of a NDE may feel himself moving very rapidly through a long dark tunnel. Drab (1981) in his (partly very questionable) study of such 'tunnel experiences' (TEs) states (l.c. p. 126) that

> *'A typical example of such a* tunnel experience *(TE) can be found in this report of a twenty-seven-year-old Englishwoman whose heart failed: 'I became less and less able to see and feel. Presently I was going down a long black tunnel with a tremendous alive sort of light bursting in at the far end. I shot out of the tunnel into this light. I was in the light, I was* part *of it, and I knew everything—a most strange feeling."*

Some tunnel experiences precede OBEs, others follow them or are simultaneous. In the paradigm case constructed by Moody the TE precedes the OBE. One way of explaining such a TE is as follows. In general it is assumed that the Shadow Matter body (including the Shadow Matter brain) of a human being is a highly elastic system (cf. Wassermann 1993). This tends to be in a contracted state when it is not attached to the ordinary matter body via its normal bonds. In a NDE, or otherwise, the bonds between ordinary matter body and Shadow Matter body 'snap'. If the snapping occurs first in the head region and proceeds towards the feet, then the Shadow Matter body (including its Shadow Matter brain) contracts (elastically) from head to feet.

It may be assumed that at the start of the contraction of the Shadow Matter body the latter splits near the top of the skull. It splits into one thin Shadow Matter body layer which remains attached to the skull, and the remainder of the Shadow Matter body then separates from this 'thin layer'. The friction involved in the separation process then heats up the separating Shadow Matter systems. While the heat can diffuse through the large contracting Shadow Matter body, this does not apply to the heat diffusing through the 'thin layer'.

In consequence of this the 'thin layer' begins to heat up and ignite and gives rise to the bright light. However, before the bright light ignites, the contracting Shadow Matter body has already fully contracted, and the Shadow Matter eyes which have moved with that body, and the Shadow Matter brain, can then perceive the glowing 'thin layer' as the bright light, at a distance.

Following this elastic contraction, and as a result of it, there occurs an elastic expansion of the contracted Shadow Matter body. During this the Shadow Matter eyes, and most of the expanding Shadow Matter body often move towards (i.e. in the direction of) the 'thin layer', giving the sensory experience of moving towards the bright light. Thus, contrary to Drab (1981, p. 147) that 'the experience of moving through a tunnel-like space is merely an hallucinatory creation of the mind, this is totally contradicted by my theory. Why, indeed, should so many tunnel experiences be similarly structured, as a result of hallucinations. This would demand that widely different human experiencers should all hallucinate the same experiences? (notably the same class characteristics).

In the present theory the 'tunnel' is not a hallucinated entity. It is a real structure, namely *the interior human body* through which the human Shadow Matter body moves during contraction and expansion. During contraction the tunnel is dark, because the bright light near the top of the skull is not yet alight. Only when the Shadow Matter body is fully contracted will the light be fully ignited. Again Blackmore (1993, p. 67) cites a case from Irwin (1985, p. 175) describing the experience of a person who had been given carbon dioxide gas. The patient reported

> '*I seemed to see a bright white light at the end of a long tunnel, and had an intense feeling that it would be wonderful if I could only reach it. I couldn't get to it before the effects of the gas wore off*'.

Blackmore (1993, p. 67) also notes that 'Tunnel experiences are not confined to dangerous or near-death situations. In fact, they appear in a bewildering variety of conditions and are one of the commonest forms of hallucinations.' This, however, is not accepted by the present author. Earlier in this section I argued that tunnels (although occasionally of hallucinatory origin) are, as a rule, unlikely to be 'forms of hallucinations'. Although hallucinogenic drugs can produce tunnel experiences, it does not follow that TEs are more than very occasionally produced by hallucinogenic drugs. According to the present point of view, most of the kinds of tunnels considered here are not hallucinatory. I have already argued, repeatedly, that there exists a great temptation of many investigators of normal and abnormal mentality to attribute anything they cannot understand to 'hallucinations'. I consider this as a cardinal mistake.

Usefully Blackmore (1993, p. 73) drew attention to Drab's (1981, p. 130) statement that 'extreme physiological stress may be especially conducive to tunnel experiences'. In fact, sufficiently strong physiological stress could lead to the separation of bonds between the ordinary matter body and the Shadow Matter body, thus leading to the initiation of a TE. I noted earlier that according to my theory in an OBE the bonds linking the Shadow Matter brain and the ordinary matter brain snap.

Hence, significantly, similar mechanisms seem to be involved both in OBEs and in TEs. If so, a considerable part of a NDE seems to involve the same kinds of mechanisms, thus leading to a partially unified explanation. That such a 'unified' (or rather partially unified) mechanism could explain parts of a TE and an OBE in similar terms makes good sense of Blackmore's (1993 p. 73) statement that 'Drab (1981) found the tunnels were often associated with out-of-body experiences. This association is well known (Blackmore, S.J. (1982) *Beyond the Body*, London, Heinemann).' Also Blackmore (1993, p. 74) states that

'While tunnels can occur to people who are quite well, they are more common near death. Any explanation of the tunnel must account for this.' In fact my present explanation can readily account for this. People near death are, more often than not, under bodily stress. According to my theory this could lead to the *'snapping'* of bonds between the Shadow Matter body and the ordinary matter body, resulting in the contraction of the highly elastic Shadow Matter body. This, prior to bond breakages, was extended and under stress. What happens then, according to my theory, has been described already in this chapter.

One of the Cardinal weaknesses of Blackmore's (1993) book lies in her excursions into philosophy of science, notably concerning the alleged need of a theory to predict new states of affairs or new phenomena (see Blackmore, 1993 pp. 75–76). I have already dealt with her brand of somewhat antiquated philosophy elsewhere (cf. Wassermann, 1993, p. 58) and shall not repeat what I said there, except that Blackmore's views on this topic are, in my opinion, invalid for reasons stated in my earlier book.

What happens towards the end of the TE, when, according to my theory the Shadow Matter body has again re-expanded and reunited with the postulated 'thin layer'? In some, perhaps many, cases the reunited system may have a measure of surplus energy which drives the 'completed' Shadow Matter body out of the ordinary matter body. This results, according to my theory, in an out of the body phenomenon (OBE). According to this there is a transition from TE to OBE, as is, in fact, observed in many cases.

Blackmore's weakness as regards philosophy and/or philosophy of science also surfaces on her (Blackmore 1993,) section titled '*There is a 'Real' Tunnel*' (her p. 76). She claims that she cannot test such a 'real' tunnel and therefore that it does not exist. This may well apply to the particular 'real' tunnel that she envisages (l.c. p. 77).

However, this does not apply to the 'real' flesh and blood tunnel envisaged in the present theory, namely the interior human body, which, above, I postulated as a real tunnel. Surely, Blackmore does not deny that such a tunnel can be observed and has been observed by anatomists and numerous surgeons. It looks as if

Consciousness & Near Death Experiences 87

Blackmore wishes to argue that because she cannot envisage a 'real' tunnel there cannot be any real tunnel. This could be, and perhaps is, bad wishful thinking.

My theory also readily explains why the light at the end of the tunnel can be extremely bright without hurting the eyes. If the light is emitted by the postulated 'thin layer' of Shadow Matter, then this light consists of Shadow Matter photons (=sphotons) rather than photons and these do not interact with the ordinary matter eyes but with the Shadow Matter eyes. These emitted sphotons, which do not interact with the ordinary matter eyes, therefore cannot hurt these eyes, notwithstanding that the light emitted by the 'thin layer' may be of high intensity.

It can be seen, by comparison, that Blackmore's theory differs drastically from the present one. She claims also (1993, p. 81) that anoxia plays a leading part in producing the tunnel. By contrast I have already argued, earlier in this book (Section 1.3), following Fenwick, that anoxia is quite unlikely to play any role in the NDE. Blackmore (1993, p. 81) also mentions that certain kinds of tunnels do not move with the eyes.

As regards the NDE tunnels this is consistent with the hypothesis that this tunnel consists of the interior human body (see above). It must also be stressed that the experienced tunnel of the TE results according to the present theory as the Shadow Matter brain moves through the space of the tunnel, and results from activation of that Shadow Matter brain via the Shadow Matter eyes.

There are also other theories of the tunnel, like that of Cowan (1982, see also Blackmore, pp. 81 ff for a simplified version). Perhaps the main weakness of Cowan's theory, compared with the present one, is that it does not explain how and why the tunnel experience (TE) is sometimes, perhaps not infrequently, related to the out of the body experience (OBE).

Some readers, unfamiliar with the properties of Shadow Matter, might wonder how a human being's Shadow Matter body can pass through the tunnel. This is filled with all sorts of structures of the human organism. However, in Kolb *et al* (1985) and Wassermann (1993) it was already pointed out that, according to Shadow Matter theory, Shadow Matter can pass unhindered through ordinary matter. However when suitably matching matter encounters Shadow Matter the latter can form complementary bonds with the former. The preceding explanation suggests, therefore, how Shadow Matter of a person can pass unhindered through the ordinary matter tunnel.

Those who, in my opinion mistakenly, believe that in Cowan's fashion (see above) a tunnel could be created by means of ordinary brain machinery, and explained simply in terms of neuroscience, might have similar beliefs concerning OBEs. Yet, no neural theory of OBEs has emerged so far. On the contrary, I have argued earlier in this chapter that OBEs involve a separation of the Shadow Matter brain from the ordinary matter brain.

According to my theory the speed of movement of the Shadow Matter body of a person down (or up) his tunnel could vary from individual to individual. It could depend on the degree of 'liberation' of the Shadow Matter body through breakage of bonds between the latter and the ordinary matter body. If many, or most, bonds are broken, we could expect a fast movement of the Shadow Matter body through the tunnel, while breakage of relatively few bonds could lead to a slow movement through the tunnel. In other words the amount of friction, which inhibits motion, between the Shadow Matter body and the ordinary matter tunnel depends on the number of bonds existing between Shadow Matter body and tunnel.

The actual experience of the tunnel in the TE could be produced by the Shadow Matter eyes of the Shadow Matter body receiving sphotons from the tunnel (i.e. Shadow Matter photons).

As regards the colour of the bright light at the end of the tunnel, there are somewhat differing reports. However, the predominant report is that by Fenwick (1991) who, on the basis of a massive survey claims that the experienced colour is either white or yellow (l.c. p. 1). This is certainly consistent with the postulated ignition of the 'thin layer'. Nevertheless, more rarely, other colours also appear. But such exceptions may not be very significant, but cannot be completely ignored.

Most electric light bulbs, depending on their wattage, also emit light that is perceived as 'whitish' or 'yellowish'. Here too, as in the case of the thin layer, we have a high degree of heating up of a material substance.

I conclude that, according to my theory, at the start of a NDE the subject's Shadow Matter body splits into two parts: (1) a thin layer which remains bound to the 'top' (say the top of the skull) of the ordinary matter body. (2) The remainder of the Shadow Matter body. This, in near darkness, or, more likely, total darkness descends down the tunnel ('up' and 'down' being here terms of convention). It also dissociates from its bonds with the ordinary matter body. The compression of this large Shadow Matter body is due to stored elastic energy being released. When compression is complete, a reactive event series occurs, with the contracted Shadow Matter body re-expanding and moving up the tunnel towards the thin layer. During this upward movement the thin layer reaches ignition temperatures (at the start of the upward movement). It is then perceived by the Shadow Matter eyes and Shadow Matter brain of the Shadow Matter body as the light at the end of the tunnel.

3.3 Back to Moody's idealized Account of a NDE

At this stage it may be useful to see how many of the NDE aspects of Moody's passage cited earlier can by now be accounted for in terms of the present Shadow Matter theory. Of much importance is the explanation of the long dark tunnel, given above, which seems to explain (apart from subjective aspects) the physical aspects of the tunnel and much of the TE. The theory also explains the buzzing noise, as due to the snapping of bonds between the Shadow Matter body the ordinary matter body and the effect of this via intermediate systems on the Shadow Matter brain.

In cases where the out of the body experience (OBE) follows the tunnel experience (TE) it was shown that the OBE can be explained in terms of the present theory (see also Wassermann, 1993). The seeing by the experiencer of the OBE of his own body from the outside and the frequently reported upward floating were explained earlier in this chapter (the upward floating had not been explained in Wassermann, 1993). Moody notes that the OBE percipient 'notices that he still has a 'body', but one of a very different nature and with very different powers from the physical body he has left behind.'

According to my theory (see also Wassermann, 1993) the 'body' of the percipient during the OBE is the Shadow Matter body. Most significantly the present theory links up the tunnel and its properties and the TE with the OBE. In this way one obtains a unification of various phenomena within the theory. In fact, the experiencing of two kinds of bodies during an OBE, namely the ordinary matter body (which is perceived from the outside) and a second body is consistent with the present interpretation of the second body as a Shadow Matter body.

Thus, quite contrary to Blackmore (1993, cf. her page 114) my theory asserts that we each have a Shadow Matter body in addition to our ordinary matter body. During an OBE the Shadow Matter body (or a part of it) leaves the ordinary matter body, remaining residually attached to the latter by a Shadow Matter cord. Also, after death the Shadow Matter body separates completely from the ordinary matter body and survives. Some of this is elaborated in the present book, some in Wassermann (1993). In contrast to this Blackmore states (1993, p. 114).

> *'I want to be quite clear. It is my contention that there is no soul, spirit, astral body or anything at all that leaves the body during NDEs and survives after death.'*

Yet Blackmore does not at all explain the upward floating that occurs in many OBEs, and which is here explained by an upward floating of the partially detached Shadow Matter body. Even more significant is the fact that in an OBE the percipient can see his ordinary matter body from the outside. According to the present theory this happens because the Shadow Matter body moves outside the ordinary matter body. It can then with the help of the Shadow Matter eyes and the Shadow Matter brain perceive the outside of the ordinary matter body. This occurs from a position that corresponds to the position of the Shadow Matter body relative to the ordinary matter body. By contrast, Blackmore simply cannot explain how and why an OBEr can perceive the outside of the ordinary body.

Blackmore (1993, p. 115) true to her dogma, assumes that imagery (and other forms of mentality) are vested in the ordinary matter brain even during an OBE (and during a NDE of which that OBE is an aspect). By contrast I assume that imagery and all mentality are rooted in the Shadow Matter brain. Thi is the case while the Shadow Matter brain is bound to the ordinary matter brain and while the Shadow Matter brain has moved out of, and away from, the ordinary matter brain. In other words it is assumed that the Shadow Matter brain is always the organ of mentality, in normal conditions and in OBEs.

Thus, according to this theory, memory is located in the Shadow Matter brain normally and during the OBE. This can explain also why the OBEr can form new memories during the OBE and recall these after the OBE has ceased. Thus, memory and other kinds of mentality are not part of the ordinary matter brain. In normal cogitation memory and mentality are also mediated and produced by the Shadow Matter brain. This acts similarly, while out of the body during an OBE. In fact, OBEs provide the best pointers to the hypothesis that ordinary matter brains, while important mediating systems between environment and Shadow Matter brain in

Consciousness & Near Death Experiences 91

ordinary perception they need not be, and presumably are not, the systems that store memories and other forms of mentality.

Blackmore's different views on this topic pertain to a traditionalism that may be totally misguided, and probably is. The assumption is that memory, mentality etc. are vested not in the ordinary matter brain but in the Shadow Matter brain of the Shadow Matter body. This is consistent with explaining the OBE as due to the Shadow Matter body and its Shadow Matter brain leaving the ordinary matter body. This assumption, as was shown earlier in this chapter could also explain very simply why in many OBEs the OBEr experiences himself as floating upward.

This could be readily explained by assuming that in an OBE the Shadow Matter body, when outside the ordinary matter body drifts upwards on account of mechanisms that I discussed earlier in this book. I do not think that Blackmore can explain any of this mechanistically. Instead she resorts, repeatedly, to mentalism of a very feeble (perhaps naive) kind, which certainly does not satisfy the present author.

Blackmore (1993, p. 115) writes as if it is a truism that memories are localized in the ordinary matter brain. Yet she does not explain how OBErs form memories during OBEs. Likewise she does not seem to appreciate the problematics of the view that engrams are located in the ordinary matter brain (cf. Lashley (1950) 'In Search of the Engram'.) It remains, of course, to be shown by further research that the difficulties raised by Lashley disappear completely when engrams are assumed to be located in the Shadow Matter brain.

In Moody's idealized account of a NDE (the 'composite account') it is stated that at some stage of the NDE the NDEr is overwhelmed by intense feelings of *joy, love and peace*. These feelings, when they occur in a NDE, are abnormally intense, and apparently leave a lasting impression on the experiencer. Blackmore (1993, p. 94–95) is trying to argue 'that the direct cause of such blissful feelings is to be found in the physical processes of the dying brain.' This assertion is here completely repudiated.

My model of the NDE does not assume that the intense feelings (of joy, love and peace) when they occur in a NDE are properties of the ordinary matter brain, let alone of the ordinary matter dying brain. It assumes that these feelings, like all meditations are properties of the Shadow Matter brain, irrespective of whether the ordinary matter brain, to which the Shadow Matter brain is bound, is dying or far from dying. In everyday feelings of joy, love and peace these sensations are assumed to be localized in specific regions of the Shadow Matter brain.

During NDEs, when these feelings become intense, it is assumed that the Shadow Matter brain regions concerned become abnormally strongly activated. Perhaps because of augmented bonding of the Shadow Matter brain regions concerned to particular corresponding regions of the ordinary matter brain.

Earlier I cited Fenwick's (1994) note that Blackmore 'suggests that the feelings of joy and bliss which are the central point of the NDE are due to the release by anoxia of endorphines. These are opiate-like chemicals known to produce feelings of tranquility.' Following this passage Fenwick duely demolished Blackmore's endorphine theory.

I shall now, briefly, discuss a short passage in Blackmore's (1993, p. 106) book, which may help to cast fresh light on the association of the feeling of peace with OBEs and many, perhaps most, NDEs. Blackmore writes

> '... *Psychologists Gabbard, Twemlow and Jones found that peace was part of the general pattern of out-of-body experiences [OBEs] and was not specific to the near-death situation (Gabbard et al 1981). It also occurs in almost all NDEs, including falls that result in no injury, or NDEs occurring during extreme stress and fear but without any physical harm. Confirming this, Owens, Cook and Stevenson found that positive emotions occurred roughly equally in NDErs close to death and those who were not (Owens et al 1990).*'

According to my theory this can be explained as follows. In an OBE the Shadow Matter body, including its Shadow Matter brain (or, perhaps in certain cases, just the Shadow Matter brain, cf. Wassermann, 1993) become detached. They become detached from the ordinary matter body, except for a residual attachment to the ordinary matter body by means of the thin (Shadow Matter) cord. The Shadow Matter system then floats upwards. It is assumed that the (possibly partly) isolated Shadow Matter brain, when separated from the ordinary matter brain is no longer subject to the stresses of previous attachment to the ordinary matter brain. It can, in this state, allow those Shadow Matter brain regions that represent 'feelings of peace', when activated. to become activated. Thereby feelings of peace arise.

Similar mechanisms could apply to the production of feelings of joy and love during the OBE. Since in many, possibly most, NDEs there occurs an OBE, the latter could give rise, by the mechanisms stated, to the feelings of peace, joy and love. These mechanisms do not involve Blackmore's postulated endorphin mechanism which, because of Fenwick's strictures, is unacceptable. (I must also remind readers that the Shadow Matter brain, invoked above, is, according to my theory equivalent to a material soul.)

Moody, in his idealized account of a NDE notes (see above) that the OBEr in a NDE 'notices that he still has a 'body', but one of a very different nature and with very different powers from the physical body he has left behind.' In the present theory this 'body' is identified with the Shadow Matter body.

Up to this stage my theory does not require any hallucinations in order to explain the heard buzzing, the dark tunnel and the OBE aspects of the NDE. At this stage it must be remembered that according to my theory it is the Shadow Matter brain that stores engrams, produces thoughts (etc.) and *not* the ordinary matter brain. In an OBE (say of a NDE) the Shadow Matter brain becomes detached (or partially detached) from the ordinary matter brain. Then a hyperactivation of some of the stored engrams of the Shadow Matter brain could occur.

This could result in the manufacture of phantasies, leading to the seeing of dead relatives or friends. It is here that we move into the realm of hallucinations. What is, however, not clear is why the hallucinated things should be people, and, more specifically, relatives and friends who have already died. Even if we assume that these relatives and friends survive, then what does survive is very likely their Shadow Matter bodies, but not their ordinary matter bodies. We know perfectly well that when an atomic bomb was dropped on Nagasaki in 1945 that the ordinary matter bodies of many people partly, or completely, disintegrated. If these 'dead' people survived it would be, according to the present theory, their Shadow Matter bodies, including their Shadow Matter brains. And Shadow Matter bodies cannot be expected to look like the ordinary matter bodies to which they formerly belonged. At any rate what survives of people could be their Shadow Matter bodies and also the memories of these people by others in the form of engrams. When Mr. X dies then engrams that he has induced while alive in the Shadow Matter brains of other people may survive. But, all this does not explain why in an OBE the persisting engrams formed by dead people while alive should become

94 Gerhard D Wassermann

hyperactivated, when hosts of different kinds of engrams could be hyperactivated instead. Why not an engram of your dog, or of the interior of a former house you have lived in?

One important possibility is that the Shadow Matter bodies (or, perhaps, *copies* of the Shadow Matter bodies) of people we knew surround us. When our Shadow Matter bodies (and their Shadow Matter brains) separate from our ordinary matter bodies then the following may happen. These Shadow Matter bodies, perhaps particularly the Shadow Matter brains, may become more accessible to the surviving Shadow Matter bodies (or their copies) that surround them. Much more accessible than they were while the OBEr's ordinary matter body was bound to the Shadow Matter body.

When this happens the surrounding Shadow Matter bodies of friends could combine with, and hyperactivate, existing engrams. Namely engrams that resemble (i.e. are complementary to) the surviving Shadow Matter bodies (or copies of them) of dead friends or other dead people known. So here we have one mechanistic possibility of explaining this aspect of Moody's idealized account of a NDE.

Next, in Moody's 'composite' case, is the 'being of light'. Perhaps this could be explained, at least partly, in a way similar to the explanation I gave of the bright light at the end of the 'tunnel'. It could be assumed that the 'being of light' is due to a partial or complete temporary splitting of a part of the Shadow Matter brain, followed by a glowing of the fracture (or split) region which is experienced as the Being of Light.

Blackmore (1993) in her entirely different theory of NDEs has suggested a different interpretation of the 'Being of Light'. She writes (l.c. p. 201): 'Perhaps the 'Being of Light' is myself. In fact in any materialist view of the NDE it simply must be, because, there is no other outside force or entity that it could be. Maybe at some level I am or could be magnificent, golden, awesome, loving and unconditionally accepting.' *Pace* Blackmore, to me the preceding conclusions and views are a non-sequitur. This does not mean that, apart from what I have postulated above about the 'Being of Light', I can provide anything fully satisfactory, although her assertion seems to *explain* nothing, in a scientific way, about the 'Being of Light'.

Next, let me turn to the 'life review' which, according to Moody (cited above) is an 'instantaneous playback of the major events of [the NDEr's] life.' I offer the

Consciousness & Near Death Experiences 95

following explanation of the playback. According to my Shadow Matter theory, memories (in the form of engrams) are not stored in the ordinary brain (although I assumed this in an earlier brain-model (Wassermann, 1978)). They are stored in the Shadow Matter brain.

In a serially ordered memory sequence it may be assumed that the engrams involved are serially ordered. Also during memory recall of a serially ordered memory sequence, the recalled memory items, i.e. the sequentially ordered engrams, are reactivated in the order in which the engram sequence was originally formed. During an NDE, the bonds between the Shadow Matter brain and the ordinary matter brain become weakened and slack. Particular engram sequences of the Shadow Matter brain could then be reactivated vastly more rapidly than in normal engram recall activity of the Shadow Matter brain. This could be the basis of the almost 'instantaneous' playback of major events of the NDEr's life.

Blackmore (1993, p. 183) quotes a very famous life-review case history, namely that of Sir Francis Beaufort 'who narrowly escaped drowning in Portsmouth Harbour in 1795. (See also Noyes, R. and Kletti, R. (1977 'Panoramic memory: a response to the threat of death' *Omega 8*, 181–94, from whom Blackmore cites her passage). Readers are advised to read either Blackmore's account of the case history or that given by Noyes and Kletti. The trouble with reported so-called life-reviews is that although the subjects may claim that they experienced their whole life passing by, this simply cannot be checked. It may not at all be true. Since we, who read their accounts do not share their memories (i.e. engrams) and have no access to their engrams in the present state of science and/or medicine. Accordingly claims relating to the extent of life-reviews may be grossly exaggerated. In fact, few, if any, of us can ever recall *normally* much of our past life, although serial recall occurs normally.

For instance, many of us can recall in correct serial order all the words of a learned poem, even if the latter is very long. Concert pianists can recall in the minutest detail all the items of a piano sonata in correct serial order. Here, according to my theory a suitable representation of the sonata exists in the Shadow Matter brain. Then, *via* the Shadow Matter brain, it activates the ordinary matter brain and, *via* this activates appropriate muscles (e.g. of the fingers). Although we can be sure that there exist engrams, we know very little about the dynamics of engrams in the recall of ordinary memories, let alone in the recall that occurs in the life-review.

In some cases (cf. Blackmore 1993, p. 184) memory recall within a life-review does not seem to be serially ordered but the recalled items seem to occur simultaneously. This could be due to the simultaneous reactivation of large numbers of engrams. There is also evidence that in some life-reviews there occurs not a serial ordering of picture-representing engrams, but a serial ordering of concept-representing engrams (which some people describe as 'thoughts', cf. Blackmore (1993, p. 184)). It also seems, judging by the evidence of some cases, that a particular life-review sequence can be triggered by a particular question.

All this is consistent with the hypothesis that the life-review, and all kinds of cognitive activities that relate to it, are synthesized by the Shadow Matter brain. I am ascribing all these powers not to a mysterious 'mind', which I repudiated already, but to the activities of a very material Shadow Matter brain. (I believe also that the Shadow Matter brain, partly via the ordinary matter brain, and partly via the Shadow Matter body can influence the immune system in disease, and could thus account for the roots of psychoneuroimmunology.)

At this stage let me cite a typical life-review from Moody (1976, p. 66). He writes:

'The things that flashed back came in the order of my life and they were so vivid. The scenes were just like you walked outside and saw them, completely three-dimensional and in color. And they moved. For instance when I saw myself breaking the toy, I could see all the movements. It wasn't like I was watching it all from my perspective at the time. It was like the little girl I saw was somebody else, in a movie, one little girl among all the other children out there playing on the playground. Yet, it was me. I saw myself doing these things as a child, and they were the exact same things I had done, because I remember them *[italics are the present author's].'*

Although this is not partly an OBE it bears some slight resemblance to a mixture of an OBE and other elements within a life-review. Whether my mechanisms for the OBE apply here is not clear, but cannot be ruled out. Indeed, according to my theory, an OBE involves separation of the bonds between the ordinary matter brain and the Shadow Matter brain. The life-review is assumed to involve a weakening of the bonds between Shadow Matter brain and ordinary matter brain (p. 98). So we have a partially common mechanism.

The character of the life-review can vary considerably between experiencers. Let me cite Moody (1976, p. 65). 'Some of those interviewed claim that, while they cannot adequately explain it, everything they had ever done was there in this review—from the most insignificant to the most meaningful. Others explain that what they saw were mainly the high-lights of their lives. Some have stated to me that even for a period of time following their experience of the review they could recall the events of their lives in incredible detail.'

Let me comment on Moody's passage, just cited. Those who claim that in their review there was everything there they had ever done could be, and probably are, totally mistaken. There could be many things they have done, which they normally cannot recall and which also do not surface in the life-review although they may exist as engrams. So to claim that a life-review comprises in some cases a recall of all memories a person has ever formed, seems to me plainly absurd.

It is, of course, a remarkable aspect of ordinary memory that we can often remember vast numbers of events in our lives in minute detail and recall them. There is, however, also forgetting, although we do not know for sure whether forgetting is absolute (destruction of memories, perhaps as in Alzheimer's disease) or merely a failure of memory recall. The remarkable thing about the life-review is not its relation to our normal machinery for remembering, but the enormous speeding up of this memory recall.

Possibly the intrinsic property of the Shadow Matter brain is its capacity for enormously fast recall and serially ordered recall. For ordinary purposes, however, this may be far too fast, so that mechanisms evolved which allow a slowing down of memory recall in everyday life. The primordial, very fast, memory recall occurs then only in NDEs or related phenomena. Some life-reviews seem to be 'directed' by a 'Being of Light' while other life-reviews proceed autonomously without a Being of Light (cf. Moody, 1976, p. 68).

In some, possibly many, NDEs the tunnel experience seems, terminally to link with the life-review. Thus Moody (l.c. p. 69) quotes from a case history, as follows. 'After all this banging and going through this long, dark place, all of my childhood thoughts, my whole entire life was there at the end of this tunnel, just flashing in front of me.' The next case, cited by Moody (1976, p. 69) also seems to involve the

98 Gerhard D Wassermann

'tunnel' as a 'completely black void', and, again, it links with the life-review. Moody (1976, p. 69) reports the description of a very sick man.

He stated that 'I found it impossible to move. Beyond that, I found myself in a completely black void, and my whole life kind of flashed in front of me. It started back when I was six or seven years old . . .'. Among other things the percipient mentions that, as regards the life-review, 'I saw only the high points, but it was so rapid it was like looking through a volume of my entire life and being able to do it within seconds. It just flashed before me like a motion picture that goes tremendously fast, yet I was fully able to see it, and able to comprehend it. . . .'

There is also evidence, consistent with my theory, that the enactment of a life-review strengthens the engrams on which that review is based (cf. Moody, 1976, p. 70 for related descriptions). Hence the percipient of the review can, after returning to normal, provide a much improved account of things that happened to him in the past, i.e. the 'normal' recall facility is much enhanced.

Moody (l.c. p. 71–73) cites two other life-review cases. In the last of them (l.c. p. 72) the life-review percipient states, among other things, that in his review he 'only saw certain things, the high points.' This suggests strongly that this review, and probably most other life-reviews are very incomplete and do *not* activate all engrams (or memories) of the percipient, but only a selection of memories.

3.4 Further Explanation of the Machinery of the Life-Review

If, as I have suggested, the life-review dynamics is based on the dynamics of the machinery of engrams, then this has some important implications, which I shall now explore. Memory sequences can be activated in the forward direction from earlier to more recent memories. Alernatively they can be activated in the backward direction from memories of recent events, via intermediate memories to memories of long past events. Clearly, when a concert pianist plays a sonata from memory, then he recalls its memorized items in a forward direction.

On the other hand, we can, often, with difficulty, recall a memory sequence in reverse order. For instance, the numbers 1 to ten can be recalled in reverse order 10, 9, 8 . . . etc. Memory of the letters of the alphabet can be activated in reverse order starting with 'z' and proceeding z, y, x etc. Again, someone can drive his car via a complex route from *A* to *B* and, in many cases, he can also move along the same route from *B* to *A*, perhaps making use of appropriate memory cues. This capacity of making use of serially ordered memories in forward or backward order becomes very relevant if, life-reviews are based on serially ordered engram sequences. If these can also be activated either in the 'forward' direction or the 'backward' direction, then this could explain some of the facts mentioned by Blackmore (1993) and others.

For instance, the famous life-review of Sir Francis Beaufort (see above) is a backwards review (Blackmore, 1993, p. 184). Other life-reviews, cited in the literature of the subject, proceed in a forward direction. Thus in relation to the life-review cited by Moody (1976, p. 66), Moody writes that the percipient reported 'I thought, "Gee, what is going on?", because all of a sudden, I was back early in my childhood. And from then on, it was like I was walking from the time of my very early life, on through each year of my life, right up to the present.'

So here we have clearly a 'forward' proceeding sequence. This can be interpreted as a serially ordered engram sequence which is recalled in the forward direction of time. All this is consistent with the hypothesis that life reviews (at least most of them) make use of engrams and the mechanisms that (although unknown) can order engrams serially. These permit engrams to be reactivated serially either in the 'forward direction' (of advancing time) or in the 'backward direction' of time (from the present, say, to an earlier time in our lives). Thus, so far the dynamics of the life-review is consistent with the dynamics of engram reactivation in either forward or backward serial order. Also the dynamics of the life-review is consistent with the hypotheses that the life-review is based on serially ordered engrams.

My hypothesis which interprets normally existing engrams as forming, in many cases, basic components of the life-review can also explain another feature of some life-reviews. Blackmore (1993, p. 184) mentions that in some life reviews 'the recollections do not flow in order at all but seem to be presented, somehow all at once.' For this state of affairs there is, again, an analogous situation in certain engram systems. It must be remembered that many engrams (and the memories they represent) are not serially ordered but form 'static' assemblies of engrams. In fact, if we look at a stationary object, then this may form in many, or possibly most or all, cases an assembly of coherent stationary engrams within the postulated

Shadow Matter brain. For such a 'static' assembly of engrams there may not exist serial order mechanisms that could activate engrams of the assembly in serial order. Thus, I conclude that there could be a close analogy between engrams and certain units of the system that produces life-reviews (presumably in the Shadow Matter brain). Perhaps the simplest hypothesis is that adopted here, namely that the basic units of the life-review system are existing (and newly formed) engrams.

I must now turn to another important point of the present theory of the life-review. I shall approach it in a slightly round-about way. Back in 1978, I published a model suggesting how the brain works (Wassermann, 1978, *Neurobiological Theory of Psychological Phenomena*, London Macmillan). This model was based on molecular biology and went reasonably far, but could not explain paranormal phenomena. To make up for this serious shortcoming I developed a new theory which dealt on a large scale with brains and psychic phenomena (G.D. Wassermann, 1993 *Shadow Matter and Psychic Phenomena*, Oxford, Mandrake of Oxford).

What led me to this new theory? In 1985 Kolb, E.W., Seckel, D. and Turner, M.S. published a paper in the leading scientific journal *Nature* (vol. *314*, 4 April 1985, pp. 415–419, titled *'The Shadow World of Superstring Theories'*). In that paper Kolb *et al* suggested that apart from ordinary matter of which, say, our atoms, our trees, our motor cars etc. etc. are composed there could also exist another kind of matter which they called Shadow Matter.

It occurred to me about 1987 in a flash of inspiration that Shadow Matter could, perhaps, play a central role in explaining paranormal phenomena as well as major aspects of a physically based psychology. I wrote up a preliminary report of my new theory in a short paper and sent it to the distinguished philosophy of science journal *Inquiry*. They soon accepted it (G.D. Wassermann, 1988, 'On a physical (materialistic) theory of psi-phenomena based on Shadow Matter,' *Inquiry 31*, 217–22.) Not surprisingly, there were neo-Cartesian (strongly anti-materialistic) Interaction Dualists, who would dearly have liked to have seen me and my new theory dispatched to Mars in a space craft, and remain there indefinitely.

According to the new theory every human being (and *mutatis mutandis* for animals and plants) consists of an ordinary body and its ordinary brain (as studied by anatomists and physiologists [etc]) and, in addition, a shadow matter body, including a shadow matter brain. The shadow matter brain is, normally, assumed to be attached to the ordinary matter brain and is assumed to be the seat of mentality, e.g. the locus where cognitive processes proceed, in particular where memories (in the forms of engrams) are stored. Thus, unlike traditional theories where engrams are assumed to be stored in the ordinary matter brain, in this theory engrams consist of Shadow Matter and are stored in the Shadow Matter brain.

One among many reasons that prompted me to postulate the Shadow Matter brain are out-of-the body experiences (OBEs). My theory assumes that normally mentality is *localized* in the Shadow Matter brain (cf. Section 2.4) and that the Shadow Matter brain can activate the body's behavioural systems via the ordinary matter brain with which it interacts. Earlier in this book I rejected the view that mentality is non-localized in favour of its localization.

According to my view each individual's mentality is fully localized within his or her Shadow Matter brain. In an OBE the Shadow Matter brain can temporarily separate from the ordinary matter brain. It can carry with it its owner's mentality, including all stored engrams, which are assumed to be stored in the Shadow Matter brain. Thus memories remain localized within the Shadow Matter brain even when the latter leaves the ordinary matter brain during an OBE.

There are people who have, not very successfully, attempted to deal with aspects of the NDE in terms of the ideology of Rupert Sheldrake (1981). I am sure that Sheldrake's views on philosophy and science are not shared by too many people (cf. Maddox 1981), certainly not by me. One of his central beliefs is that there exists such a thing as 'morphic resonance'. He thinks that most animals of the same species (and likewise plants of the same species) are closely similar in their anatomy and physiology because there exists a 'morphic resonance' This exists between different organisms of the same species. That the similarity of organisms of the same species could be vested in their genomes and the genes that compose the genomes has apparently not occurred to Sheldrake. He disregards genetic developmental programs. I have certainly followed a different path. First in a book '*Molecular Control of Cell Differentiation and Morphogenesis*' (Wassermann 1972 New York, Dekket) and, in a much improved version, in a paper by Clowes and Wassermann (1984) and Wassermann (1997) together with a new theory of plant morphogenesis (Wassermann, 1997).

In my theory of morphogenesis (cf. Wassermann, 1997) I have shown how appropriate genes could systematically provide for developmental programmes. This could lead to an organism (usually) with the characteristic structure and functions of the species concerned. Variations of structure and function are attributed to variant genes, so-called alleles of the organism. So, for all this one does not need Sheldrake's 'morphic resonance' but can proceed within more or less orthodox biology.

There are also various people who believe that they can apply the obscure notion of 'morphic resonance' as an explanatory tool in parapsychology and in relation to NDEs. I do not think that morphic resonance is needed at all to deal with the paranormal.

Instead, I have been inspired by the interesting paper by Kolb *et al.* (1985) in the prestigeous journal *Nature* (London). This proposed that in addition to ordinary matter (composed of atoms etc.) there could also exist another type of matter which they term 'Shadow Matter'. Inspired by this notion, I showed in much detail in an earlier book (Wassermann, 1993) that many phenomena of parapsychology could be explained in terms of postulated properties of Shadow Matter (Wassermann, 1993). All these large numbers of explanations, and others given in the present book, do not require 'morphic resonance'. It thus, becomes as redundant in parapsychology as in the more orthodox 'normal' (e.g. biological) sciences.

It seems to me that Kolb *et al.*'s notion seems to get one much further than Sheldrake's ideology. There are undoubtedly people, who, like Blackmore (1993, p. 199), claim that Sheldrake's idea 'seems to give a scientific basis to the idea that we are all connected, that each of us is not alone but part of a greater whole.' This connectedness, however, does not have to invoke 'morphic resonance'. It could be explained by means of the 'normal' mechanisms of verbal (etc.) communication and by means of telepathy. This could be accounted for by Shadow Matter theory (Wassermann, 1993) without falling back on obscure 'morphic resonances'.

I do not find some of Blackmore's views, vis-à-vis Sheldrake's theorizing, more convincing than Sheldrake's own ideas. For example, she writes (Blackmore, 1993, p. 200), 'with our increasing understanding of neural networks it is clear that a biological system can create its own notions of similarity on the basis of very simple principles. When a neural network learns to associate two patterns of firing with each other it is found that similar patterns will evoke similar responses in terms of patterns of firing. . . .'.

Whether artificial neural nets, currently being studied and, indeed, studied already several decades ago are suitable systems for cognitive representation is highly debatable. In my earlier book *Neurobiological Theory of Psychological Phenomena* (Wassermann, 1978, London, Macmillan) I have submitted in chapter 6 of that book many neuropsychological theories, including various kinds of neural nets, to extensive criticisms. I believe that some, perhaps many, of my criticisms of neural nets of Wassermann (1978) also apply to the, allegedly, 'simple' neural nets discussed by Blackmore in the passage cited above. Such simplistic neural nets simply cannot cope with the very intricate performance requirements that an adequate model of the brain has to satisfy, and readers are referred to my extensive criticisms of neural nets and other kinds of models of brains and the criteria to which such models can, and have been, submitted (Wassermann, 1978).

Nevertheless, there could be various models of brains that could cope with the notion of 'similarity' in mechanistic terms, even if this does not act as a prop for the utility of 'morphic resonances'. Let me explain. But before I give my explanation let me first deal with the reason for the similarity of organisms of the same species (notably human monozygotic twins). This similarity does not depend on 'morphic resonances'. It does not mean, as Sheldrake wishes to convince us (cf. Blackmore, 1993, p. 199) that 'Like influences like'.

The reason why two human monozygotic twins are as similar as they are has nothing to do with 'morphic resonance' between them. Instead it is vested in the similarities of their genomes (= genetic systems). For each particular allele of a particular gene of one of the twins there exists an allele of the same kind of the same kind of gene in the other of the twins. To understand why this is so, the reader has to consult works on molecular biology. But the reader does not have to resort to 'morphic resonance'. That apart from the presumed 'identity' of the genomes of the 'starting cells' of two monozygotic human twins there exist also other pointers to genetic determination of twins in the following passage taken from Needham (1942, p. 230).

'. . . *According to Davenport (1920), the production of human identical twins appears with great frequency in certain families, and may therefore be connected with a specific gene or gene-group. Against this there is the conclusion of Greulich's recent review that only dizygotic (fraternal) twinning in man is hereditary. But for birds it has been shown by Byerly & Olsen (1934) that the incidence of twinning varies according to the breed, a fact which will be difficult to explain on other than genetic lines.'*

Although Needham's book is bound to be dated, I am confident that the essential points made, relating to twinning, are likely to remain. They show that twinning and the genomes of twins are a matter of molecular genetics (which did not exist when Needham wrote his (1942) book). But they are not a matter of obscure 'morphic resonance'. The preceding arguments suggest that *similarities* of monozygotic twins are vested in genes and do not result from 'morphic resonances'. Sheldrake disregarded the important role played by genes in morphogenesis. *Pace* Blackmore (1993, p. 199) there are good reasons to think that Sheldrake's beliefs have dismayed modern developmental and molecular biologists. Certainly my own work suggests that there are good reasons for thinking so (cf. Clowes and Wassermann, 1984).

This, let me add, is not the end of Sheldrake's 'natural philosophy.' I read Sheldrake's (1981) book some three or four years ago, and shall not re-read it. Instead I shall rely on Blackmore's (1993, p. 199) summary of some of his ideas. She believes that Sheldrakes theory seems to make possible telepathy and clairvoyance. This may well be so. Yet, my totally different theory of paranormal phenomena, which is based on Shadow Matter (Wassermann, 1993) also explains large chunks of paranormal phenomena. These include telepathy, clairvoyance and OBEs, *inter alia*.

Now let me return to where I departed from models of brains. I noted that there 'could be various models that could cope with the notion of 'similarity' in mechanistic terms.' As in Wassermann (1978) it may be assumed that there exist two kinds of engrams (or possibly even more kinds). The first of these are engrams of patterns which impinge on our sensory systems (e.g. retinae, tongue, ears etc.). The second variety of engrams encode concepts not in a concrete way but in the guise of symbolic kinds of structures. Suppose now that we look at a banana. Then, *via* intermediate channels of the ordinary matter brain this could lead to the activation, in the Shadow Matter brain, of a sufficiently matching engram of the first kind. It could represent a banana, or several different such engrams.

Because of the deformability of Shadow Matter (owing to its postulated elasticity) the Shadow Matter engrams that represent bananas can be deformed until one or more of them fits the presented Shadow Matter representation of the banana. (In the same way, because of the elasticity of Shadow Matter engrams, the following could happen. There could be myriads of Shadow Matter representations of the same letter written in myriads of different hand-writings. These could be made to match a relatively small number of engrams by appropriate elastic deformations and fitting of these engrams.)

Suppose now that (in my model) a pattern-representing engram is bound to a concept-representing engram. Thus, for instance, a particular banana could activate pattern-representing engram(banana) if an appropriate pattern-representing engram exists. This, in turn, could activate the concept (banana)-representing engram bound to that pattern (banana)-representing engram, thereby evoking a conscious representation of that concept.

There could be many variants for the pattern banana on many different pattern (banana)-representing engrams. These could match different varieties of bananas, and become activated when particular bananas are presented. When one or more of the pattern (banana)-representing engrams are activated, then the associate concept (banana)-representing engram(s) could become activated.

Different Shadow Matter brains of different people could represent similar patterns (eg. variants of a banana) by means of similar pattern (banana)-representing engrams. Whereas the pattern-representing engrams for sufficiently similar patterns of different Shadow Matter brains are assumed to be closely similar, this need not apply to the concept-representing engrams. Thus, different people's Shadow Matter brains could represent the same concept (e.g. 'banana') by means of different concept-representing engram structures. Hence X, when seeing a particular banana, perceives this (when suitably presented) as the concept 'banana'. Y, when seeing the same banana (when similarly presented) perceives this also as the concept 'banana', but represented by a different engram structure.

The model, as just presented, could explain perceptual similarities in simple cases without invoking Sheldrake's notion of 'morphic resonance', which I reject quite generally. I believe that it is not very difficult to enlarge, substantially, my model of pattern and concept perception. This can be done so as to apply to quite advanced perceptual generalizations or 'similarities' without invoking 'morphic resonances.' Brain (1951, p 23) has illustrated such generalizations in the following passage, which I have cited in several of my books. It presents the central issue of 'stimulus equivalence' by splendid illustrations:

> *'When someone speaks and another person listens it may seem a very simple process, but in fact, it is so extremely complicated that it is very difficult to understand. Let us take as an example the word 'dog'. No two people pronounce the word 'dog' in exactly the same way, yet we always know what it means. Not only that, it can be sung, shouted or whispered and it still conveys the same thing.'*

> *'But we can go further than that. The written word 'dog' will still mean the same thing, though the word no longer consists of sounds, but is made up of black marks on a white piece of paper: it can still be understood, whether it is written or printed, in large or small letters, in black or coloured type and in any sort of handwriting short of complete illegibility: in many handwritings the marks that people make on paper have very little resemblance to the letters they are supposed to represent. Here, then, there is as great a variety among the visual patterns presented to the nervous system as among spoken words.'*

Brain mentions that the sense of touch provides similar generalizing capacities in pattern recognition. 'The reader of braille can recognize a series of raised pimples on the paper, which make a pattern quite unlike ordinary letters, and yet also mean the word 'dog'.' Additional elegant examples of a related kind are presented by Neisser (1967, Chapter 3) and by Fodor (1968, pp. 24–30). Such power to generalize could hardly be expected to depend on 'morphic resonance', which is a cliche that does not account for the great variety of stimulus equivalence in human pattern recognition.

The preceding is cited from Wassermann (1974). In Wassermann (1993, p. 78) I added, 'Stimulus equivalence also exists for many animals (e.g. rats, see

Lashley (1960)). If the human perceptual system did not have the capacity to recognize and classify equivalent variants of stimulus patterns as being equivalent, then we could not recognize most, if any, objects.

The retinal image of objects may vary in position on the retina, vary in shapes projected by the objects on the retina, vary in retinal size, colour etc. Hence all these give rise to appropriate variations in the activated patterns of nerve cells within the ordinary matter brain. Yet, despite this, these greatly varying nervous activity patterns can lead to the correct allocation of equivalent patterns to the same concept (or class).'

These formidable equivalences do not only turn up with respect to stimulus equivalence. They also surface in relation to motor equivalence. Let me quote some typical examples of motor equivalence. We can write our signature, with all its typical bends and twists, with a pen held between thumb and first finger of the right had, or between thumb and first finger of the left hand, or held in the right or left fist.

We can also write our signature with our right or left toes on a plot of sand, or with a pen held between the right big toe and its neighbouring toe or the left big toe and its neighbouring toe. Or we could fix a big pen to the right fore arm or the left forearm, or we could use a pen fixed to our forehead, and so forth. Also each signature thus written could be written in large letters or smaller letters.

All this seems most unlikely to be explicable in terms of Sheldrake's notion of 'morphic resonance', despite the similarities of the resulting signatures. In each case cited, systems of muscles are used which differ from the systems of muscles used in the other cases cited. Indeed, large numbers of different, appropriate combinations of muscles could produce the same signature, when allowed to handle a suitable writing instrument. Thus, motor equivalence is almost as versatile as stimulus equivalence. If Fenwick thinks that parts of, or the whole of, the NDE is an enigma, then, surely, motor equivalence and stimulus equivalence seem, at least to me, to be equally big enigmas, at least at present. This, however, does not justify the invocation of an even bigger enigma, namely 'morphic resonance'.

3.5 Some Views on the Nature of Powerful Scientific Theories

Blackmore repeatedly pontificates on what, in her opinion, constitutes a good scientific theory, and I have written much on the structure of scientific theories (Wassermann, 1994). I have also contributed myself to scientific theorizing in various fields of science, and since I disagree thoroughly with Blackmore's views, I must state my credentials, as far as they are relevant.

I have lectured extensively at undergraduate level at Newcastle upon Tyne University in classical mechanics, electromagnetic theory and at undergraduate level and M.Sc. level in quantum mechanics. I have published in theoretical optics; in theoretical biology (genetic control of developmental events; evolutionary mechanisms). I published also in philosophy of mind; in philosophy of science and general philosophy and in parapsychology, among others.

Blackmore (1993), in common with various people who have not made a special study of the philosophy of science, claims (her p. 195) that 'to be of any use, a theory must provide testable predictions'. In contrast to this *ad hoc* statement, which I reject, I wrote in Wassermann (1993, p. 58) that

> *'I think that the dated view that 'testing' of scientific theories amounts always exclusively to verification (or else falsification) of 'predictions' of theories, can be discarded (see also Wassermann, 1989 and Wassermann, 1974, section 3.12). A scientific theory can be tested often by demonstrating the validity of its explanations as well as its predictions (if these exist). A good many years ago I quoted Professor Hans Jürgen Eysenck (Wassermann, 1974, p. 123). Eysenck (1953, p. 235) argued [quite mistakenly] that it is 'not* ex post facto *explanations which constitute science, but predictions which can be verified.'*

Yet, following Eysenck, the retrospective explanations [i.e. *ex post facto* explanations] given by Einstein's theory of the photo-electric effect are science. So are explanations of Bardeen *et al.*'s theory of superconductivity [superconductivity and many of its facts had been known long before Bardeen's theory]. So are the explanations given by Felix Bloch's theory of electronic conduction in metals (see below). These and many other explanations provided by many other scientific theories on a retrospective basis, form essential aspects of science. Eysenck, who [was] a prominent psychologist, started his career by studying physics. Surely he must [have known] that explanations play a central part in physics and many other sciences?

On the same page of Wassermann (1993) from which I have just quoted I also wrote, preceding the passage already quoted:

'One way of testing my integrated theory of psi-phenomena is analogous to the way in which one has 'tested' many theories in physics. This is by using these theories to explain *many already known phenomena, and by examining how these theories fit the phenomena. For instance, in 1905 Einstein explained the already known photo-electric effect, but did not predict it. His explanation also 'tested' Planck's earlier assumption of the existence and properties of light quanta (i.e. photons). Thus, Einstein explained the photo-electric effect by making assumptions about the properties of photons.*

Likewise, the theory of superconductivity of Bardeen and his associates (e.g. Cooper) [The late Professor Herbert Föhlich contributed a key idea to the current theory of superconductivity (see his obituary in The Times (London) *30.1. 1991 p. 16] explained the already known phenomena of superconductivity, but did not predict them. Again, Felix Bloch established a well known quantum theory of electronic conduction in metals, which explained many already known facts and laws (e.g. Ohm's Law) without predicting them. Einstein, Bardeen and Bloch (etc.) obtained Nobel Prizes for their respective explanatory feats listed, showing that explanations are highly valued in science, at least as much as valid predictions. Successful explanations serve as strong tests of a theory even if (like predictions) they cannot prove a theory to be true.'*

I conclude that Blackmore's view that 'to be of any use, a theory must provide testable predictions' simply did not apply to the theories mentioned. For these people obtained Nobel Prizes, after the time these theories were put forward as explanations. I simply do not know how familiar Blackmore is with theoretical physics. But let me stress that, *pace* Blackmore, my theory of the life-review in NDEs is *explanatory and not predictive*.

Blackmore is, perhaps, on firmer grounds when she claims that a good theory should be specific (Blackmore, 1993, p. 194). Indeed, for a theory to explain something or to predict something, that something has to be specific. For instance, Einstein's explanation of the photo-electric effect dealt with something specific, namely the postulated photon and its postulated quantal energy (among other things).

Perhaps it could be argued that *any* theory, to be ranked as a theory, has to deal with some specific things (e.g. the periodic table in chemistry in as much as it can be ranked as a 'theory'). Nevertheless, one may be tempted, as Blackmore seems to be (when it comes to explaining the NDE) to demand that any theory that explains essentials (of the NDE) should also explain a host of 'specific phenomena'. This may not cut out the theory in its present state. Thus Einstein's theory of the photo-electric effect could not explain certain aspects of quantum electrodynamics which could only be explained many years later, after quantum mechanics and quantum electrodynamics were born.

Blackmore (1993, p. 195) also claims that allegedly 'A good theory does not invent extra realms, 'other worlds' or new forces or energies without very good reason and without providing independent evidence that they exist. A theory that builds on well-understood principles is to be preferred to one that invents new ones *ad hoc*.'

Here again we have sufficient evidence that Blackmore is apparently not really familiar with the great theories of physics, to which her polemics does hardly apply. I mean, for instance, the electromagnetic theory of Maxwell, the General Theory of Relativity of Einstein, the non-relativistic quantum mechanics of Schrödinger and the relativistic quantum mechanics of Dirac. All these theories were built on new *ad hoc* principles rather than on well-understood principles. If Blackmore's 'philosophy of science' had been adopted by Maxwell, Newton, Einstein, Schrödinger, Heisenberg, Dirac and countless others we would now be without a host of mighty theories. All of these theories and many others (e.g. quantum electrodynamics (Dirac), quantum chromodynamics Gell-Man's theory of quarks (for which he obtained a Nobel Prize)) were based on new principles created *ad hoc*. Here Blackmore seems to exhibit clearly that she is not familiar with some of the finest creations of science. Likewise, the great theory of evolution, put forward by Sir Charles Darwin was not built on well-understood principles but on new *ad hoc* principles (e.g. the novel notion of 'natural selection').

In view of the preceding conclusions concerning Blackmore's philosophy of theory construction and earlier, partly related, views by Eysenck, I have not adopted their points of view nor have I adopted the views of like-minded numerous other theorists. Their dogmatic opinions simply do not harmonize with the practices of scientific theory construction of numerous theorists, including some prominent people.

4 The Conjectured Nature Of Survival

4.1 The likely Immortality of the Soul

According to the present mechanistic theory of psychic phenomena which was first developed in my earlier book (Wassermann, 1993) man has a material soul which is equated with the Shadow Matter brain. Normally the Shadow Matter brain (which is composed of Shadow Matter) is bound in a quite specific manner to the ordinary matter brain which is familiar from anatomy. During out of the body states the Shadow Matter brain can become detached from the ordinary matter brain. More generally, in many, or most, out of the body states the complete shadow matter body could become detached from the ordinary matter body. However, during life it is assumed that the Shadow Matter body remains residually attached to the ordinary matter body by a thin elastic cord, composed of Shadow Matter.

At death the Shadow Matter body (including its Shadow Matter brain) could become completely separated from the ordinary matter body and the thin cord could become severed. So, what survives is the Shadow Matter body, including its Shadow Matter brain. By hypothesis, mentality, including all memories and cognitive activities, is normally not transacted by the ordinary matter brain. This just serves to link the Shadow Matter brain with the ordinary matter body and, indirectly with the outside world. Mentality is, in my theory, transacted by the Shadow Matter brain. Hence, when, and if, the Shadow Matter brain survives at death it can continue to transact mental processes. Since in my mechanistic materialistic theory consciousness is due to epiphenomena of Shadow Matter states of the Shadow Matter brain, consciousness can persist in the surviving Shadow Matter brain.

Thus, according to the present theory, the 'seat of consciousness' is not the ordinary matter brain, but the Shadow Matter brain. This could not only explain why we may remain conscious after death, but it may also explain why people claim to remain conscious in 'out of the body experiences' (OBEs). In fact the widely claimed existence of OBEs seems to be closely linked with the machinery that operates in survival after death. During death, in many cases, the ordinary matter brain may be partly or completely destroyed by accidental causes, or in death the ordinary matter brain may more slowly decay. Yet, all this, according to my theory, does not apply to the Shadow Matter brain. Also the surviving Shadow Matter body may experience a turnover of its Shadow Matter, thereby renewing its Shadow Matter by Shadow Matter constituents that surround the Shadow Matter body. (In fact such a turnover could also be expected to occur during life, just as the ordinary matter brain experiences replacement of its ordinary material constituents, e.g. indirectly via the food that we eat, the air we breath etc.).

Although, to the best of my knowledge, Shadow Matter (and a soul composed of Shadow Matter) was not known to the ancient Greeks, the notion of a soul was certainly familiar to them. Thus, Bowker (1991, p. 63) notes that 'the actual inscription on Plato's tomb makes the same point: 'Earth in her bosom here hides Plato's body, but his soul has its immortal station with the blest.' So here, as an important aspect of Plato's philosophy we have an immortal soul (although, presumably, not made of matter) linked, during life, to a mortal ordinary body. It must, however, be stressed that survival of the soul does not necessarily imply immortality. For all we know survival may only involve a finite time span, although this need not be so.

It is obvious that the Greeks could not have known the immortality of the soul nor could anyone else. They could have known mediumistic pronouncements (etc.) which they interpreted, as many present-day people do, as indicators of survival which does not imply survival for all eternity, although this possibility cannot be excluded either.

After an out-of-the-body experience (OBE) the percipient of the OBE may remember what he experienced during the OBE. Since, by hypothesis, the Shadow Matter brain (=soul) is the seat of memory, it follows that during OBEs the partially or nearly completely detached Shadow Matter brain (i.e. the material soul) can form new memories. Similarly the soul could form new memories when surviving death, and, according to my theory, the ordinary matter brain does not form memories either when alive or dead.

4.2 Personal Identity during Life and Death

It has long been recognized that *some* of the key elements which encode our personal identity are our genes. These genes, together with the food that we take in, determine the hardware of our ordinary matter bodies, notably the proteins, that, directly or indirectly, constitute our bodies. Our personality has long ago been thought to be encoded by our ordinary matter brains as well as by the somatic constituents on which the ordinary matter brains act. Accordingly, it was generally believed that when we die our personality dies.

Contrary to this view the hypothesis of this book assumes that much of our personality is encoded by our Shadow Matter brain, and that when the ordinary matter brain dies the Shadow Matter brain survives, becoming detached from the ordinary matter body, and with it part of our personality survives. Of course, only certain essential parts of our personality survive. Thus, much of our ordinary matter body perishes at, or after, death and much of that ordinary matter body (e.g. tongue, eyes etc.) normally contributes to the somatic expression of our personality.

When the ordinary matter body dies then, by hypothesis, the surviving Shadow Matter body (and its Shadow Matter brain =soul) can still express a sizable aspect of the former personality, which we may call the surviving personality. This surviving personality includes our memories our ability to feel and see (with the help of Shadow Matter eyes) to perceive things, our cognitive abilities, and so forth.

Our finger prints, like our personal identity, of which they are a part, are unique. The environmental influence during development undoubtely plays a prominent role in shaping our personal identity. Yet the particular combinations of the existing alleles of some 100,000 genes which we have inherited are more decisive in making us (normally) look and behave like members of our species than (say) the food we eat. (Cf. monozygotic twins, notwithstanding the drastic differences of memories of these twins).

Many believers in parapsychology (but not all of them) believe that the personalities of living people can communicate with the surviving personalities of the dead. The communication could take place *via* telepathy between living Shadow Matter brains (i.e. souls) and surviving souls. There are, however, problems. Why can surviving souls communicate so rarely, if ever, anything truely important or original, and why do they not inform us what sort of world they live in? Indeed, many or most of the 'messages' which spiritualist mediums claim to receive from the dead are utterly trivial ('aunt Flora is here with flowers for you').

Possibly the communication by telepathy between a surviving soul and a living soul may be no more effective than telepathy between living souls (which is very limited). Indeed, if telepathy between the living were as effective as speech or sign language, then few people would ever question the reality of telepathy. The machinery of telepathic communication (cf. Wassermann, 1993) may simply be underdeveloped compared to normal forms of human communication.

It remains, however, possible that telepathic communication between surviving souls is much more effective than telepathic communication between surviving souls and living souls. One reason for this could be that living souls are bound to ordinary matter brains (by hypothesis), which need not apply to most surviving souls (but see my discussion of reincarnation in Chapter 5 below). This bonding of living souls may largely inhibit living souls from receiving telepathic input from surviving souls.

With respect to personal identity it is important to distinguish between genes and gene expressions. Our personal identities consist not just of our innate endowments, our capacities to walk, to read and write, to talk and think in idiosyncratic ways, but consist also, at least for many people, in a creative capacity. We can discover problems and often solve them. What makes a great mathematician is his capacity to discover or spot important problems and to solve them, often, in his idiosyncratic style. A great singer, like Placido Domingo, has not only got his characteristic voice but also his particular mode of interpreting the music he sings. All this is part of personal identity. I suspect that our (assumedly) surviving souls can still solve problems, although this is uncertain.

Problem solving may depend on the use of our limbs and other bodily components, it may depend on the use of auxiliary material hardware such as paper, ball point pens, computers etc. Much of human expression depends on vocalization (in speech and singing). All these are merely randomly selected aspects of personal identity. While a surviving soul may remember songs heard

Consciousness & Near Death Experiences

and, perhaps, invent new songs, it obviously cannot sing. Yet, by telepathy, a song remembered by my soul could be communicated to other souls.

The idiosyncratic style in which we communicate depends not just on our ordinary matter brains but, I believe, primarily on our Shadow Matter brains (= souls). Even surviving souls could recognise each other by their surviving style of communication. The capacities to have feelings and moods are, according to my theory, located in the soul and survive with the soul. Thus, all aspects of mentality (including cognitive capacities) are supposedly located in the soul and could survive with it. Accordingly a major portion of human personal identity (but not all of it, e.g. not the capacity to move our muscles, not our facial expressions) could survive.

Another prominent aspect of personal identity is its purposefullness, i.e. its feature of goal seeking. This, too, could be expected to survive with the soul. More generally, all features that this theory tends to ascribe to the soul are here hypothesized to be survivable with the soul.

But what about the souls of murderers? I believe that there are genes (or rather alleles of genes) for criminality. This is suggested by the various individuals who are serial killers or criminals like Hitler. Yet, I do not know to what extent criminality is inheritable. If it is notably inheritable then the criminal trait, where present, would be represented in, and survive with, the soul. However, since surviving souls lack motor apparatus (e.g. limbs, tongues etc.) to execute crimes, they are no longer able to translate their surviving criminal tendencies into crimes.

But could surviving souls undergo change and 'improve'?

4.3 Indefinite Evolution of Surviving Souls

Mentality could have evolved as follows. Biological evolution (partly steered by TIMA, cf. the TIMA theory as presented by Wassermann 1997) could have produced an evolution of ordinary matter brains. These, in turn, could have co-produced and evolved Shadow Matter brains (= souls) which are the seats and producers of mentality. According to this view souls (=Shadow Matter brains) and mentality coevolved.

The preceding theory assumes that surviving souls by using their existing Shadow Matter, and by accretion of additional Shadow Matter from the Shadow Matter 'ocean' (see above), could interact *via* telepathy. In this way any one surviving soul could *via* telepathy receive information from other surviving souls and store this information by its memory system and also interact with this information. Likewise, surviving souls could, *via* telepathy, exchange (reciprocally) information with souls of living people.

On the one hand this could explain information that trance mediums claim to receive from surviving personalities (or souls). On the other hand it would suggest an indefinite evolution of surviving souls. Consider the system of interacting surviving souls, interacting souls of living people and interacting surviving souls interacting with souls of living people (and *vice versa*). This could form the physical basis of what the psychiatrist Carl Gustav Jung called the 'collective unconscious' (except that souls may be conscious). Thus, one function of biological evolution is to have evolved human brains and their Shadow Matter brains (= souls). This, in turn, could have led to the evolution of the collective unconscious, an evolution that is still going on. (Perhaps it would be best, in future, to refer to 'the collective conscious' instead of 'the collective unconscious').

By producing ever more surviving souls, ever more novel ideas can be generated in the hereafter. These can telepathically influence souls living on Earth (and also the souls of astronauts in space), thus augmenting constantly the realm of mentality. When the solar system, as now known, ultimately ceases to exist, and the Earth with it, surviving souls could continue to survive, and evolve. Similar soul-evolving, and soul-surviving processes could have occurred (or could occur in future) on other planets of other stars throughout our galaxy and other galaxies.

It seems reasonable to assume that many or most lower species also have souls (i.e. Shadow Matter souls = Shadow Matter brains) which have coevolved with their nervous systems.

4.4 The Importance of Spontaneous Cases

There are various parapsychologists, even some prominent ones, who seriously believe that one should disregard spontaneous psychic phenomena. These include out-of-the-body experiences (OBEs) and near death experiences (NDEs) and concentrate on experimentally produced data only (e.g. such as described in Radin's (1997) excellent book. The exclusion of spontaneous data in Radin's book is hailed by R.S. Broughton's review of Radin's book. The review is titled 'A Milestone on Parapsychology's Long March' Network, April 1998 No. 66, pp. 57–

59. Broughton's absurd view stems from the opinion that spontaneous phenomena are devoid of scientific contents. I repudiated this view in my book (Wassermann, 1993), where I tried to show that many spontaneous phenomena can be scientifically explained.

By contrast Broughton (1998), in his review of Radin's book, considers it a virtue that in Radin's book 'there are no ghosts or poltergeists, or near-death studies or out-of body experiences—just a hard-hitting, fresh presentation of the best experimental evidence and a penetrating dissection of the often bogus criticisms that sceptics have used to impede progress in the field.' *Pace* Broughton if, as I have demonstrated in Wassermann (1993), out-of-the body experiences (and, likewise, near death studies) are essential for understanding the putative mechanisms of psi-phenomena, then it is hardly a welcome step by Radin to have ignored these phenomena.

In his review of Radin's book Broughton asks why the sceptics keep up their onslaught on parapsychology. To this question Broughton also supplies the answer (l.c. p. 59) when he states that in Radin's book 'The chapter entitled 'Theory' does not offer any . . .'. So here one has the old shortcomings of experimental parapsychology: it is a heap of facts without an explanatory theory. Many people say that this is just not science since any respectable branch of science requires a body of theory. Hence, the sceptics, mistakenly believing that there is no theory in parapsychology, continue their onslaught.

Contrary to these sceptics and many anti-theoretical parapsychologists my book (Wassermann, 1993) provides a comprehensive theory of psi-phenomena, a theory mainly based on spontaneous phenomena, trying to explain the mechanisms of such phenomena. That Radin and Broughton have completely ignored my novel mechanistic materialistic theory may have to do with the widespread absurd anti-materialistic bias of many or most parapsychologists. Many of these people do not realize that materialism is not the same as bolshevism.

If theorizing in parapsychology is rightly and naturally related to spontaneous phenomena (see Wassermann, 1993) then it is not wise of Radin (as Broughton (1998, p. 57) claims) to limit his focus to the experimental side of parapsychology (which in his book does not yield a theory).

Lest it be thought that my Shadow Matter theory of Wassermann (1993) only deals with spontaneous psi-phenomena, let me stress that the theory also explains much else. It explains telepathy, clairvoyance, precognition and possible survival after death. It, thus, is a theory that can explain the phenomena dealt with in Radin's book as well as spontaneous phenomena, ignored by Radin.

4.5 The Targeting of specific other Souls

If souls are to communicate with each other, say, in the hereafter by telepathy, then telepathic signals from any particular soul must be able to reach most or all other souls and interact with them. If so, the soul of any living person could by telepathic signals communicate with the souls of most or all other living people. Likewise, any surviving soul could by telepathy communicate with any other surviving soul. Also any surviving soul could by telepathy communicate with all sufficiently receptive souls of living people.

The telepathic mechanisms that could achieve this were suggested elsewhere (Wassermann, 1993) and will not be repeated here. Thus, a theory of the mechanisms of telepathy is essential for explaining how the souls of living people or the souls of living people and surviving souls could communicate. In this context it is relevant to note again that Radin (1997)—notwithstanding all the applause by Broughton (1998)—has not put forward theories of mechanisms of any psi-phenomena. Such as telepathy, clairvoyance, out-of-the-body experiences etc.

That any aspiring theory of telepathy must contain theories of mechanisms whereby one soul can communicate with any other soul seems as obvious as some of the mode of functioning of a large telephone exchange system. In such a system each telephone can contact every other telephone (though not simultaneously, since there are 'engaged' signals possible for any receiver). Such a state of affairs need not apply to more versatile souls, where any one soul could *simultaneously* interact telepathically with vast numbers of other souls.

Examples of where such simultaneous mass communication occurs are well known on Earth. Typical is a political meeting, where a single speaker addresses a large audience. In this case a speaker's soul could via the ordinary matter brain of the speaker. This could lead to the activation of the ordinary matter brains of members of the audience and, hence, to activation of their Shadow Matter brains (=souls).

4.6 Locations of surviving Souls in Heaven and Hell A 'Dual Hereafter Theory'

I believe, rightly or wrongly, that nowadays many people consider the concepts of heaven and hell as somewhat naive, a view that I do not share for reasons to be explained. Earlier I assumed that after bodily death the surviving Shadow Matter body and its Shadow Matter brain (=soul) float, because of upthrust exerted on them by the Shadow Matter 'ocean' to near the top of the heavy Shadow Matter (=H-SM) ocean. This is in accordance with Archimedes' principle for fluid mechanics. This top region of the H-SM ocean corresponds possibly to what certain religions traditionally call 'heaven'. This upward floating, however, might only apply to certain classes of Shadow Matter bodies. Namely those Shadow Matter bodies whose souls had been associated with ordinary matter brains which genetically were 'normally endowed'.

By contrast it is assumed that the ordinary matter brains of criminals are genetically 'abnormally endowed'. Their Shadow Matter brains (= souls) are assumed to consist of an ultra heavy kind of Shadow Matter which is much heavier than the Shadow Matter that constitutes the 'normally endowed' Shadow Matter brains. Ultra heavy Shadow Matter bodies and their ultra heavy souls occupy, by hypothesis, a region of the Shadow Matter 'ocean' which is located below the Earth surface. This is in turn, is located below the region I have called 'heaven' and which is occupied by normal souls.

The region of the Shadow Matter ocean located well below the earth surface corresponds, perhaps, to the traditional notion of hell, and abnormal souls migrate to hell. In my model of heaven and hell, heaven and hell simply serve to separate the surviving souls of normal people from those of criminals or others with (genetically) evil dispositions. Whether surviving souls suffer in hell, and if so, as I assume, why this should be so, remains an open question. The whole metaphysics of heaven and hell is a matter of speculation, but a speculation which is close to many religious systems and sentiments.

Normal, as well as abnormal, living souls are, during life on Earth, the localities of all kinds of feelings, including pain (according to my theory). Possibly those abnormal souls that occupy hell may be under severe pressure from the surrounding Shadow Matter 'ocean', and this may, epiphenomenally give rise to feelings of severe pain.

Thus, according to my theory, there are two kinds of survival. There are Shadow Matter bodies and their souls which survive in heaven, where they have an enjoyable existence. Then there are Shadow Matter bodies and their souls which survive in hell where they suffer severe pain. But both kinds of souls survive. However, survival could be pleasurable (in heaven) or it could be an existence of suffering (in hell). The naive view of many spiritualists that we 'simply' survive after death may be grossly oversimplified since there could be different kinds of survival of different kinds of souls (in heaven and in hell, respectively). In my earlier book (Wassermann, 1993), while discussing the possibility of survival, I simply disregarded the possibility of there being different kinds of survival. I only tried to show that survival is possible within a mechanistic materialistic theory.

Although some of my hypotheses are severely metaphysical, I have left aside the widely postulated hypotheses of the existence of an only omnipotent and omniscient God in heaven and a one and only devil in hell. I have always found it difficult to understand why, if God is omnipotent, He does not simply anihilate the devil. Possibly God's omnipotence, though vast, is not total and God cannot descend to the realms of the devil. Personally I see no need to postulate either God or the Devil, but I am not a militant aetheist and do not wish to stop others from believing in God.

In my model there exists certainly a kind of omniscience, whereby any one surviving soul could telepathically communicate its encoded knowledge to every other surviving soul. Conceivably this exchange of knowledge may only be confined to souls in heaven, but it could also apply to souls in hell, and possibly all souls in heaven might exchange knowledge with all souls in hell. But this seems unlikely, particularly, as stipulated, heaven and hell are separated domains. Take the case of Adolf Hitler whose soul would certainly survive in hell where it would be submitted to extreme torture (which epiphenomenally would be experienced as severe pain which might last indefinitely). It seems reasonable to assume that no soul in heaven would want to exchange telepathically information with the soul of Hitler (and the souls of similar criminals) in hell, and would not accept any incoming telepathic message from hell by not being 'tuned' to telepathic messages from hell. The inmates of hell, by being in immense pain, might have no inclination to communicate with each other.

Souls, both in heaven and in hell, could be gradually modified by the pressure of the surrounding heavy Shadow Matter ocean in which these souls are immersed (by hypothesis). Thus, souls could become lighter with time and float upwards. In this way souls in hell, which have become sufficiently modified could slowly float upwards to heaven, where these souls are surrounded by lighter layers of the Shadow Matter ocean.

As mentioned, above, in my earlier book (Wassermann, 1993) I simply assumed as one possibility that all souls (= Shadow Matter brains) survive. This led to the faulty conclusion that the souls of super-criminals like Hitler, Himmler, Eichmann, Goebbels Goehring and their likes survived in a way similar to the souls of good people. With the introduction of two hereafters, a heaven and a hell, this leads in the present modified theory, to the possibility of a dual destination at death. Some surviving souls will populate heaven, others will populate hell.

Whether a surviving soul will go to heaven or to hell will depend on the structure of that soul. The ordinary matter brain's structure is partly determined by some of the genes (made up of DNA) of the owner of that brain. The ordinary matter brain's structure, in turn, will (by hypothesis) determine the structure of the Shadow Matter brain (= soul). Accordingly a person's surviving soul's structure is indirectly partly determined by specific genes of that person. Hence, whether a person's soul migrates to heaven or to hell depends indirectly on the alleles of the genes inherited by that person.

This harmonizes with the view that the souls of good people are partly or largely genetically conditioned and the same applies to the souls of bad people. Many readers, of course, will argue that the environment in which a person has lived on Earth is also likely to have modified the structure of his or her soul. This will raise, in a new context, longstanding disputes about whether genetic alleles or the environment are dominant in shaping personality or, in this case, the soul (= Shadow Matter brain).

Thus, whether people arrive in the hereafter in heaven or in hell depends on the makeup of their soul, this makeup being partly genetically and partly environmentally determined. If the genetically and environmentally endowed persons who are ranked as bad go to hell, then we cannot blame these people to be thus endowed. However hell may be regarded as a, possibly long lasting, purifying resort, where bad souls become gradually modified (their Shadow Matter becomes gradually transformed).

That genes are partly responsible for the makeup of our soul and our appearance etc. is suggested by the similar appearance of monozygotic twins, so that if certain genes (i.e. their present alleles) indirectly influence the soul of one of the twins then the same alleles in the other twin may also modify the soul of that twin, although the environment could have different effects on the souls of the twins.

The preceding discussion raises the issue of personal responsibility. The genetic aspect of a person's soul is innate, and a person is not responsible for it. The soul may partly determine a person's actions and if these actions are not completely genetically determined there remains the possibility of personal freedom and choice (see below). Accordingly, although people's actions are partly, or perhaps largely, under considerable indirect genetic influence we can regard people as partially responsible for some of their dispositions and actions. At least courts of law act as if this were the case. If they did not do so, then much evil in society could not be eradicated.

Although we cannot blame criminals, like Hitler, for the genetic alleles for criminality they inherited, we can blame (i.e. attribute personal responsibility to) these criminals for the use they made of these genetic alleles. They could only be absolved from blame if their actions were *entirely* gene determined. This, however, seems quite unlikely, because people have the capacity to think and to make decisions. Our thoughts may be partially genetically determined, and they are partially environmentally determined and partially by memories. These factors, and others, raise the issue of personal choice.

4.7 Do Souls have a personal Choice?

Serial killers, like the 'Yorkshire Ripper' Peter Sutcliffe, and mass-murdering monsters like Adolf Hitler (who ordered the mass murder of 6 million Jews in World War II) have, according to my theory, a grossly abnormal soul (= Shadow Matter brain). Hitler not only murdered millions of Jews, but he instigated murderous wars against Russians, Americans, Poles and many other nations. Sutcliffe murdered preferentially women. Hitler, because of the pathological structure of his soul, may only have had a limited choice of victims for murder, and, likewise Sutcliffe.

The alleged choices (i.e. freedom to choose) of people (and their souls) may be illusionary. But this brings us back to the question of human responsibility. If people are driven to their actions by their souls and their somatic endowment then their main instruments of choice are likely to be their souls. While choices do genuinely occur all the time (at least in the author's opinion), personal responsibility may amount to no more than saying that souls primarily determine our actions and that souls *are* responsible for our actions (which are assisted and executed by our bodies).

But if souls (= Shadow Matter brains) are made of Shadow Matter, then what is it about souls that determines their choices and responsibilities? We cannot do without the concept of responsibility. Otherwise we could not try to sentence criminals. If habitual criminals like Hitler have or had (like all of us) partially genetically determined souls, then it is these genes which partly or largely or completely determine their responsibilities. Thus, if we imprison a criminal it is to protect society from the possible actions controlled by some of his or her genes. Some people say that imprisonment is punative retribution for crimes committed. But if some people inherit genes for criminality then locking away should not be regarded as punishment but as protecting society. Even if souls of criminals have a more limited choice than souls of normal people then this is no reason for not imprisoning criminals to protect society.

4.8 The Problem of Evil

In the preceding sections of this chapter I have already directly or indirectly dealt with some aspects of the problem of evil. Here I propose to carry the discussion further. I argued that surviving souls of evil people go to hell, because of the structures of the alleles of certain soul-determining genes that these evil people possess. Some of the soul-determining genes of evil people can, *via* the soul, jointly with other soul-determining systems lead to evil deeds of these people.

Thus, I suggest that evil people are born evil (and good people are born good). However the environment in which they live could sometimes reduce the increasing tendency towards wickedness of evil people, or in some cases the environment of evil people could augement their wickedness. These environmental influences would be transcribed in the soul as memories (engrams). I have already argued that we cannot blame people who are born evil for their evil disposition. This, of course, does not mean that we must not, by all means possible, combat their evil doings.

One may ask why some people are born evil and, hence, by some of the innate structuring of their souls, have their souls condemned to go to hell. Perhaps we must regard such innately evil people as (say genetic) freaks of nature. Perhaps hell, if it exists as some religions, and my model, suggest, acts as a kind of natural selection that separates the bad from the good in the hereafter (where the good go to heaven and the evil to hell, because of genetic aspects of souls). But why should the evil suffer in hell? Being innately evil do their surviving souls deserve to suffer because of the inheritance of evil dispositions? If so, then this is no more than to say that the destiny of souls in the hereafter is not a just one. Alternatively it could be argued that people born evil could combat their evil disposition.

But does any one seriously believe that an arch-criminal like Hitler would or could stop his horrendous murderous acts? One is driven to the conclusion that souls have evolved so that some of them give their owners a propensity for evil acts and that such souls go to hell in the hereafter. There they could undergo gradual modification, even if their residence there is painful to them. Perhaps we can only believe that the Earth is structured so that some people inherit evil souls and then go to hell to undergo a corrective course which modifies their souls. While the preceding views are very speculative, they seem to harmonize with the views that are upheld, in related forms by several religions.

4.9 Mentality of surviving Souls and Extraterrestrial Souls

If, as my theory of mentality assumes, souls are the carriers (or seats) of mentality, and souls survive in heaven or in hell, then surviving souls retain the mentality, or propensity for mentality that they had while their owners were alive. According to this theory the originality and creativity of certain people is carried by their soul and depends on the structure of that soul *via* the genes of its owner. The creation of important novelty, such as Bach's B minor Mass, is here regarded as due to genetically controlled creativity of the soul (= Shadow Matter brain). I believe that surviving souls that were capable of creating great works during the life of their former owners can continue to create great works in heaven (but not in hell, where the dense Shadow Matter of hell inhibits the creativity of souls).

It seems likely that there exist also souls on some planets of other stars in our galaxy and other galaxies. Indeed, some surviving souls could have migrated from planet Earth to other planets in our solar system. So souls of dead Earth inhabitants might not just survive in earthly heaven and hell but also close to other planets of our solar system (etc.). Shadow Matter could also (like a Shadow Matter 'ocean') surround the surfaces of other planets and form the region for populating the surfaces of these planets with migrant souls from Earth. These migrant souls (which might migrate jointly with the Shadow Matter bodies to which they belong) could then endow other planets with earthly mentality.

4.10 The Likely Evolution of Souls

If the existence of surviving souls in heaven is principally devoted to creativity of great original works, then inspiration of souls on Earth could in many, possibly most, cases come telepathically from souls in heaven. Thus, religious talk about the 'heavenly host' may be based on Earthly evidence of heavenly souls. Human inspiration and creativity could in some, perhaps many, cases be based on human souls receiving telepathic messages from highly evolved heavenly souls (i.e. souls which originated on Earth but evolved further in heaven). Thus, inspiration could be regarded as Earthly evidence of a more advanced kind of existence of creative heavenly souls. Heaven and its souls could be of great benefit to earthly human souls.

If people have souls then it seems likely that this applies also to many animal species and, perhaps, also to plants, although the latter possibility is more doubtful. Thus, just as there exists a Darwinian evolution of organisms, so there may exist an evolution of the souls of many, perhaps most or all kinds of organisms. The souls of higher species are assumed to be developmentally formed by the nervous systems (say ordinary matter brains) of these species. Thus, one important byproduct of the evolution of ever higher species could be the evolution of ever more complex souls which could also survive.

Whether the surviving souls of lower animals also go to heaven or hell is an open question. But if animal souls exist on Earth, as I believe they do, then those who preach kindness to animals are likely to be right. Animal souls may be endowed with consciousness, so that animals may have feelings and be conscious of the way they are treated by man and other animals. Perhaps contrary to this view is the fact that many animals kill others for food supply.

If my conjectures are correct, then consciousness has not suddenly started with man but existed already in many species throughout evolution. If so then one of the most likely significant aspects of future evolution is the future further evolution of souls of higher complexity than that of man. This (since, by hypothesis, souls are Shadow Matter brains) could be expected to depend on the further evolution of ordinary matter brains via genetic systems. Possibly there might exist coevolution of ordinary matter brains and souls. As ordinary matter brains evolve further, this leads to adaptive evolution of souls and the further use of the changing souls could (via the souls' Shadow Matter) exert stress on the ordinary matter brain. This, in turn could lead to 'pseudo-exogenous adaptations' of brains and corresponding modifications of related genetic systems. While all this is hypothetical, I believe that it is plausible.

Let me just briefly refer to pseudo-exogenous adaptations. I have discussed these at length in Wassermann (1997, 1998). Thus I wrote:

> '*Examples of pseudo-exogenous adaptations are cited by Waddington (1957, p. 160) in the following passage:*
> '*One of the most familiar pseudo-exogenous adaptations is that of the thickened skin of the soles of our feet. This thickening is obviously an adaptation to stress which this region of the body has to bear, but as Darwin pointed out, and as Semon (1913) discussed in a full-length paper, the thickening already appears in the embryo before the foot has ever borne any weight. The structure therefore cannot be a direct response to external pressure, but must be produced by the hereditary constitution independently of the specific external influence to which it is an adaptation.' How genetic systems could arise (non-randomly) to make the pseudo-exogenous adaptations hereditary was explained by Wassermann (1997).'*

4.11 Is there bodily Resurrection?

As a mechanistic materialist I do not believe in bodily resurrection. However, perhaps I may be permitted to try to throw some light on what people of a different faith or orientation think about bodily resurrection. To get an idea of what Christianity means by resurrection let me first cite S.T. Davis (1989, p. 125). He writes:

'The fathers and scholastics insisted . . . that both body and soul must be present or else the person does not exist. A man cannot be said to exist as such when the body is dissolved or completely scattered, even though the soul remains by itself—so says Athenagoros (see S.T. Davis (1989) p. 142 for reference). And Aquinas agrees: 'My soul is not I, and if only souls are saved I am not saved nor is any man' (see Davis 1989 p. 142 for reference). Thus the Christian hope of survival is not the hope that our souls will survive death (though on temporary disembodiment that is one important aspect of it), but rather that one day God will miraculously raise our bodies and reunite them with our souls.'

Contrary to this view I assume that the ordinary matter body (with its appearance, its gestures and other forms of behaviour) need not form an essential part of a person for many purposes. Instead I insist that the Shadow Matter body together with the Shadow Matter soul constitute (for many or most purposes) the essence of a person, and that after death a person's ordinary matter body is not raised in a miraculous way. Instead after death the ordinary matter body largely disintegrates (or even at death), whereas the Shadow Matter body survives and, as part of it survives the Shadow Matter soul.

Those who, like St. Paul, believe in a resurrection assume that there occurs a transformation at death (or soon after) of the ordinary matter body resulting in a new immortal 'glorified' physical resurrection body (Davis, p. 126). This transformed 'glorified' physical body is assumed to be inhabited by the same soul as inhabited the pre-transformation ordinary matter physical body. By contrast my theory assumes that the ordinary matter body is not transformed at death but slowly or quickly perishes whereas the Shadow Matter body (including its Shadow Matter soul) survives and enters heaven (or hell as appropriate (see Section 4.6)).

It is one of the postulates of Shadow Matter physics that Shadow Matter can pass freely through ordinary matter. Accordingly the Shadow Matter body of a deceased person should be able to pass freely through walls of buildings, ceilings, windows (etc.) (cf. Wassermann, 1993 p. 48).

In an article in the book edited by Stephen, T. Davis (Death and Afterlife, Basingstoke Macmillan, 1989), Kai Nielsen ('The Faces of Immortality') states (l.c. p. 2) that belief in bodily resurrection 'is a considerable scandal to the intellect.' If by bodily resurrection we mean that the whole of the ordinary matter human body which may have been cremated soon after death, or partially or completely disintegrated in a fatal accident (or by an atom bomb as at Hiroshima or Nagasaki) becomes by divine intervention, or otherwise, reestablished (as the new immortal 'glorified' resurrection body (see above), then I certainly do not believe in this. I believe, as stated, that what survives is not the ordinary matter body (unless specially preserved after death) but the Shadow Matter body including its Shadow Matter brain (= soul).

It is important not to mistake a part of supposed bodily resurrection for survival of the soul as discussed in this book. Survival could, but need not necessarily, be indefinite. To get an idea of what bodily resurrection involves, let me cite Nielsen (l.c. p. 8).

> *'Suppose Sven dies and rots and eventually turns into dust and indeed further suppose his grave gets upturned and the dust, which is all that he is now, is spread randomly by the wind. God being omnipotent, at the Last Judgement gathers these specks of dust together and reconstitutes them into an energised body that looks exactly like Sven and has all the memories Sven had . . . .'*

In the case of Sven's assumed survival (without resurrection), by contrast, Sven's ordinary matter body may well disintegrate, but not his Shadow Matter body and its Shadow Material soul, which survive. For such survival one does not have to invoke divine omnipotence, but only assumes properties of Shadow Matter. The Shadow Matter brain (i.e. the soul) must not be confused with the immaterial soul assumed by many Cartesian dualists or similarly minded thinkers. Nielsen (l.c. p. 11) writes

> *'A standard problem for any belief in an immaterial self is over how it is possible to individuate this self (distinguish it from other selves) since it does not have a body.' This problem does not arise for the present theory which postulates a Shadow Material soul i.e. a soul which is made of Shadow Matter, i.e. the soul is a self which is material.*

Consciousness & Near Death Experiences 131

At this stage let me refer to a few important sources concerning the soul, personal identity and survival, among others. These are Flew (1967, 1976), Phillips (1970), Penelhum (1970), Perry (1978) and Geach (1969), and important books on disembodied survival are also Purtill (1976), Helm (1978) and Reichenbach (1983) among others. Perry's question-raiser that we cannot observe souls does not rule out that they may exist, any more than the fact that currently we cannot observe Shadow Matter (but only infer its existence) rules out the likely existence of Shadow Matter.

Perry (1978) obviously was not aware of the possible existence of Shadow Matter, which only surfaced later (Kolb *et al.*, 1985). It is, therefore, not surprising that Perry thought wrongly that no thesis about personal survival of death via survival of the soul is coherent. This argument does not apply to a Shadow Matter brain (= soul) and its likely survival. Perry also believes that the memory criterion of personal identity is never sufficient to establish personal identity since memory is fallible. However, memory based on the Shadow Matter brain could be fallible without impairing personal identity based on the Shadow Matter brain.

Now back to Nielsen. He writes (l.c. p. 13)

'It is a rather common belief among many analytic philosophers (A.J. Ayer, Peter Strawson and Bernard Williams among them) that the very idea of disembodied person is incoherent, for reference to a body is a necessary condition for establishing the identity of a person and for ascribing identity through time to a changing person.' After an intermediate argument Nielsen (l.c. p. 14) asserts that 'the very idea of a 'bodiless individual' seems to be unintelligible.' (Penelhum (1982) 'Survival and Identity', in Mostafa Faghoury (ed.) Analytical Philosophy of Religion in Canada *(Ottawa, Ontario, University of Ottawa Press p. 14)*

Pace Ayer, Strawson and Williams and others, I do not think that the idea of a disembodied person is incoherent, if by a person's body we mean that person's ordinary matter body. As I have argued, at death the ordinary matter body could be cremated, or could otherwise disintegrate, while the Shadow Matter body (including the Shadow Matter soul) could survive. If normally much of the identity of a person is established by that person's Shadow Matter body, including the soul (see Section 4.2) then at death that person may become disembodied, in the sense that the person's ordinary matter body decays or is destroyed.

Yet, if the Shadow Matter body and its soul (with all its memories and all its cognitive capacities) survive then much of our identity as persons may survive. Thus, a person may be disembodied of his or her ordinary matter body, yet remain a person in many or most important respects. (True, that person cannot see himself or herself as a person in a mirror.) I conclude that in my theory most of one's personal identity is vested in one's Shadow Matter body (including one's soul). In contrast to this Nielsen (l.c. p. 14) claims that 'The only alternative... for in any fundamental way establishing personal identity is having the same [ordinary matter] body (bodily continuity).' I claim that most of personal identity is an aspect of the Shadow Matter body (and its soul) and not an aspect of the ordinary matter body. Thus, most of one's personal identity does not depend on having the same ordinary matter body, but on having the same Shadow Matter body.

When Nielsen (l.c. p. 16), after spinning a long yarn (about Sarah), claims that it 'makes sense to speak of a 'bodiless person'' then I am inclined to agree if by 'body' he means, as he does, the ordinary matter body. In my theory a person is (and remains in the hereafter) a person by virtue of having a Shadow Matter body and its soul (= Shadow Matter brain).

As long as the Shadow Matter body and its soul survive a person could remain a person even if that person's ordinary matter body, including its ordinary matter brain perish. A person, even if disembodied (i.e. void of the ordinary matter body, but not void of the Shadow Matter body) could still communicate telepathically (via the Shadow Matter brain) with other still embodied or disembodied persons.

A disembodied person can still see, via his or her Shadow Matter eyes and with the help of the Shadow Matter brain, the living bodies of other people but not the Shadow Matter bodies of other disembodied people.

Nielsen (l.c. p. 19) claims also that 'Person may not be a natural kind, but a human being—a human person—is. For our kind of natural kind, mind and character are dependent for their activities on a body in causal interaction with the world ((Gillett, 1986), Mackie (1985)).' *Pace* Nielsen, according to my theory mentality and character are dependent for their activities primarily on a Shadow Matter body and its soul. These, while there is also an ordinary matter body (causally in interaction with the world) may receive input from the ordinary matter body. They may psychokinetically act on the ordinary matter body (e.g. the ordinary matter brain) and, thereby, activate the ordinary matter body.

When Nielsen (l.c. p. 19) asserts that 'we have no coherent grounds for thinking ourselves to be immaterial substances or disembodied continuants incapable of destruction,' then I partly beg to differ. We certainly may *postulate* that we are not immaterial substances. We are composed both of an ordinary matter body (as described in anatomy books) and a Shadow Matter body. At death, the Shadow Matter body (including its soul) may form a disembodied continuant possibly incapable of destruction, whereas the ordinary matter body largely (or sometimes completely) experiences destruction at or after death.

Do Shadow Matter bodies and their souls survive in order to be compensated in a hereafter for the suffering and injustice (etc.) of this world? (See Nielsen (l.c. p. 20) for partly related remarks). This would contradict the notion of Section 4.8 that the souls of evil people go to hell. Conceivably hell may not be a permanent domicile for the surviving souls of evil people. The tortures of hell (pain etc.) could gradually physically modify the tortured souls. Possibly souls that are most evil would take longest to modify back to a 'normal' state. When they reach this state they could migrate to heaven.

During their process of restoration to normal, souls could become lighter, and this could induce these souls to migrate to the upper regions of the Shadow Matter Ocean (see Section 4.6), i.e. to Heaven. Thus, I envisage Hell as a soul-transforming region where some souls first suffer badly (pain) but gradually become progressively lighter and move increasingly upwards and gradually enter heaven.

Nielsen (l.c. p. 20) who, unlike Kolb *et al.* (1985), does not postulate Shadow Matter, and who does not postulate a Shadow Matter soul, believes in the 'eventual utter destruction' at or after death. Contrary to his views and conclusions I have shown here that there exist totally different possibilities. These, although not dictated by traditional religious beliefs of some faiths, harmonize in parts with long established religious notions and beliefs. I arrived at this view of heaven and hell and the migration of souls (and their survival) by certain gaps in my earlier book *Shadow Matter and Psychic Phenomena* (Wassermann, 1993). There was no 'double-hereafter' postulated, as in the present book. Accordingly in the 'single hereafter' postulated in Wassermann (1993) the souls of good people and the souls of evil people all migrated at death to the same 'single hereafter'. This could have led to a mixing of evil and good surviving souls in the same region of space round the earth. It suggested that there was likely to be a mechanism which separated evil souls from good souls until the evil souls were purified. Some important conventional religious beliefs provided already the basis of the 'double hereafter' model which is here adopted. It should be noticed that this model, as presented here, does not, unlike the teachings of the bible (etc.), postulate any divine agency (or agencies). (Indeed my model is mechanistic.)

Nielsen (l.c. p. 20) indirectly exhorts us to 'live out one's life in a meaningful and pleasant way', a hedonistic idea. Hitler and vast numbers of his fellow-criminals presumably thought that they were living a meaningful and pleasant life when they instigated and executed the unparalleled systematic murder of six million Jews. With these murders as examples of ultimate evil it seems more rational to assume that there is a hell where the souls of the wicked migrate at death.

There accompanied by immense suffering (pain etc.) these souls, through a long-drawn-out physical process, become purified. (I am almost using here language of the kind Handel used in the *Messiah*.) Very slowly they migrate to Heaven, over an immensely long period of time. This model, though closer to the ideas of some religions, is still a mechanistic materialistic model. It lacks deities and miracles and other central notions of various religions. I must stress that much, most or all of my 'afterlife model' could be dispensed with without invalidating my main theory of psychic phenomena, which is based on Shadow Matter (Wassermann, 1993 and this book).

Are those who suffered unjustly during life (e.g. from starvation, injustice, maltreatment in death camps etc.) to be compensated in the Hereafter by going to a geographically high region of heaven (see pp. 82 ff) where their souls prosper? This could depend on whether these people lived good lives. A bad person may have suffered while alive (e.g. Hitler during the final part of his life, when he saw the Third Reich crumbling into dust), yet his soul may go to hell, while a good person's soul would always go to heaven. This may seem immensely naive. Yet, it is not difficult to envisage mechanisms that in the hereafter 'scan' the souls of people in order to classify these souls according to the deeds or misdeeds they inspired during the lives of their former owners.

Consciousness & Near Death Experiences 135

It is wrong to think that all people are bad (in which case they would, after death, all go to hell). In the famed Dreigroschen Oper (three penny opera) by Kurt Weil and Berthold Brecht, Brecht produced the lines 'Der Mensch ist Schlecht' (Man is evil!). Undoubtedly many or most of Brecht's cronies were communists and many, or perhaps most, of these were bad, which, perhaps, led Brecht to his faulty conclusion.

But I do not believe that the majority of people on Earth are bad, notwithstanding that Brecht was a famed writer and poet. Many important and wicked economic or political or military decisions have been made by a single individual or a few people. Thus, the Kaiser (Wilhelm 2nd) and his Imperial Chancellor von Bethmann Hollweg together decided to enter the (1914–1918) world war which led to the slaughter of innocent millions of men. Again, Hitler ordered an army of helpers to murder 6 million Jews.

In concluding this section I must stress that one key to my theory is a duality involving on the one hand the ordinary matter body on the other hand the Shadow Matter body including its material soul. There is also a second, independently postulated duality of heaven and hell.

During an out-of-the-body experience (OBE) the Shadow Matter body, including the soul, is, by hypothesis, assumed to separate partly or largely from the ordinary matter body. This separability of the Shadow Matter body (inclusive of soul) and ordinary matter body figures centrally in my extensive preceding theory. Also according to my theory the Shadow Matter brain (= soul) is 'the essence of a person' and not the ordinary matter body, although this may also in an important way characterize that person and allow others to recognize that person on Earth. My position is not one of traditional dualism which posits a dualism of an ordinary matter body and an immaterial soul, the latter being the essence of the person (Davis, 1989, p. 120).

The soul of my theory is material, namely the postulated Shadow Matter brain. *The Shadow Matter brain in life and death is assumed to be the seat of consciousness and of cognitive transactions.* Only the ordinary matter body and the Shadow Matter body when combined form a 'complete person'. But the surviving Shadow Matter body (including its soul) form an incomplete person, but capable of carrying out great intelectual feats, if sufficiently endowed.

However, I do not believe that after death 'some time later in the eschaton God miraculously raises our bodies from the ground transforms them into 'glorified bodies' and reunites them with our souls thus making us complete and whole again' (cited from S.T. Davis (1989, p. 121) Such a view, with its implied miracles may appeal to members of certain religions but is, in my opinion, scientifically not very appealing in this day and age. In the case of bodies which at Hiroshima and Nagasaki were completely disintegrated I cannot believe that God spent his divine energy to reunite and sort out the host of separated atoms, ions molecules (or their subconstituents) into correctly matching parts of a 'glorious body'.

I think that belief in resurrection amounts for many of those who embrace this belief to a view of bodily reconstitution after death. By contrast the postulates of a surviving Shadow Matter body and its surviving soul do not require reconstitution of the Shadow Matter body and its soul after death since, by hypothesis, the Shadow Matter body and its soul never perish.

Elsewhere S.T. Davis (1989, p. 119) writes:

'One traditional Christian view of survival of death runs, in outline form, something like this: On some future day all the bodily dead will be bodily raised, both the righteous and the unrighteous alike, to be judged by God; and the guarantee and model of the general resurrection (that is the raising of the dead in the last days) is the already accomplished resurrection of Jesus Christ from the dead.'

This traditional view differs drastically from my view that the Shadow Matter body and its soul can survive either for a long time or indefinitely, whereas the ordinary matter body perishes rapidly or slowly at or after death and is never resurrected.

Significantly, J.A. Irish (1989, p. 145) writes:

'Immortality, understood as a natural survival capacity that comes with our humanity, is fundamentally incompatible with the biblical notion of death and resurrection. Professor Davis is consistent with Christian Scripture in saying 'apart from God's intervention death would mean annihilation for us' (Davis 1989, p. 119).'

Davis' conclusion need not be accepted by those mechanistic materialists who, like myself, believe in an afterlife. According to my theory, even without God's alleged intervention, death would not necessarily mean annihilation for us, since the Shadow Matter body and its assumed material Shadow Matter soul could continue to exist and function intact.

Irish (l.c. p. 147) asks:

'How long can a human being be thought of as a person without his or her body?' To which I have already replied, and now repeat: A human being can largely be thought of as a person as long as that being's Shadow Matter brain (i.e. his or her soul) survives. As long as the soul survives our memories and most or all our cognitive faculties would survive according to my theory. Irish (l.c.) also asks: 'How can we envision the unique development of personal character in a Helen Keller or an Elephant Man apart from their bodies?' Here, again, the Shadow Matter body and its Shadow Matter brain could come to the rescue. Let me stress that in my theory the soul is 'embodied' since it forms a part of the Shadow Matter body. Also, my model does not 'miraculously sustain the soul at what would otherwise be death' (Irish, l.c. p. 147). The soul, being material (by hypothesis) may continue as a material entity without divine help in the form of religiously assumed miracles.

4.12 What about 'Life' in Heaven?

A good summary of many classic arguments concerning this Section heading and/or related questions is given by J. Hick (1989). Hick refers to the possibly surviving alleged communicators as 'spirits'. He notes 'that the 'spirits' say very little about their own world and their own lives in it. We gain no impression of their activities apart from the brief periods when they are communicating with us on Earth,' [subject to some exceptions].

Now, if, as my theory suggests, many (but not all) surviving Shadow Matter bodies (including their souls) are immersed in a highly homogeneously structured Shadow Matter Heaven, then there is not much to describe. The supposedly surviving Shadow Matter bodies (including souls) of persons other than the communicator cannot be recognized (except by clairvoyance) as structures by other than inmates of Heaven (if they reside in Heaven). But the structure of these Heavenly inhabitants, being composed of Shadow Matter only gives them an appearance (to each other) which differs totally from the appearance of living people (as they appear to other living people or survivors).

Thus, the (say) heavenly inhabitants recognize each other by sight and acquired memory of what they looked like (just as we on Earth recognize many people by remembering their appearance). The heavenly inhabitants would look quite unrecognizable to a 'new arrival' from Earth. However, surviving souls in heaven could communicate with each other by telepathy. Likewise surviving souls in heaven could communicate telepathically with the souls of living people on Earth.

However, assume that the surviving communicator is sufficiently well educated. I.e. he or she has a soul which is endowed with sufficiently complex engrams, acquired while alive or during residence in the hereafter as a result of telepathic communication with the souls of other survivors. Then communication of complex conceptual notions between the surviving communicators and an inadequately endowed soul of a living trance medium (*via* telepathy) may not be possible. This may be the reason for the silence of the 'spirits' about their world.

After all, a highly sophisticated mathematician on Earth cannot describe intricate mathematical theories to mathematical ignoramuses. So how should a surviving soul of a celebrated mathematician be able to inform the soul of a mathematically uneducated trance medium about the surviving mathematician's possibly immensely complex mathematical thoughts. Moreover, communication between surviving souls and souls of living people on Earth may be harder than communication between two or more surviving souls. (Souls of living people are bound to living bodies, which may inhibit these souls in some respects, so that they may not be competent to receive complex telepathic signals from surviving souls.) I suggest that 'life' in the hereafter consists of telepathic communications between surviving souls and, perhaps, recognition of other person's surviving Shadow Matter bodies by clairvoyance.

Surviving souls in heaven could, *via* telepathy, form mutually linked communication systems and storage systems. In this way one would not require the auxillary machinery that is used on Earth to facilitate communication, such as blackboards and chalk, video and audio communication systems and much else.

Thus one soul could temporarily (by forming new engrams) act as a repository systems for cognitively produced notions of some other souls, thereby forming a holding memory. (Just as a blackboard in a class room of a school or university forms a temporary repository of communicated language or symbols (etc.)).

(In passing I must mention that the soul conceived of as a Shadow Matter brain differs completely from the soul viewed as a dispositional structure (by Hick, 1989, chapter 7), see also Nielsen in S.T. Davis (ed.) (1989) p. 200). (A dispositional structure is a property a person has, Nielsen (1989) p. 200).

Nielsen (1989, p. 201) writes, by way of rebutting Hick:

'The very idea that after death consciousness continues in an utterly disembodied state, a state Buddhists call Bardo Thödol *seems to me incoherent.'*

Contrary to this view (which *is* incoherent) I have assumed throughout much of this book that consciousness is a property of, or state of, the soul, i.e. of the Shadow Matter soul (= Shadow Matter brain). At death the material soul continues to exist and, with it consciousness.

Nielsen (1989, p. 202) also argues

'But where talk of life after death involves some claim (putative claim) to a self existing in a disembodied manner, even if only for a short time, then it seems to me that we have a notion which is incoherent.'

Now, my talk about 'life after death' is based on the hypothesis that the Shadow Matter brain (= material basis of the 'self') survives as a Shadow Material (i.e. a material) system and does not exist after death in a disembodied manner. Hence my theory about survival of the soul (or physical basis of the 'self') is not incoherent in the sense of the theories or claims that Nielsen criticized in the passage cited above.

4.13 Creation of Souls

To cite from Prabhu (1989, p. 69): 'the orthodox Christian view [is] that God creates each soul *ab initio* . . .'. This view is just another aspect of creationism, nowadays widely rejected by most life scientists. I have fairly extensively dealt with, and rejected, creationism in my book *Keys to Life* (Wassermann, 1997). In my book *From Occam's Razor to the Roots of Consciousness* (Wassermann, 1997a) I cited (l.c. p. 169) a typical onslaught by Marks (1981) which appeared in the leading scientific journal *Nature* (London).

Marks wrote:

'The creationists claim that we may come to know the Creator by deducing Him from his works on Earth. Well, we know that there are 750,000 species of insects now alive. Anyone who has ever had a conversation with an entomologist knows what a deadly dull lot those fascinated by insects can be. To envision the Creator expanding his divine energy on three quarters of a million meticulously grafted bugs necessitates an image of Him as a dismal insufferable cosmic bore!' Those who believe that God creates every soul ab initio *seem to me as misguided as those who believe that God rather than evolutionary processes created* ab initio *each of 750,000 species of insects.*

The creationist view of the origin of souls, cited above, differs totally from the present hypothesis that souls (i.e. Shadow Matter brains) develop autonomously. It is here assumed that organismic development is an autonomous process (not depending on God), whose possible machinery has, at least partly, been modelled by Clowes and Wassermann (1984). As the ordinary matter human brain develops the Shadow Matter brain (= soul) is assumed to develop concomitantly, remaining attached to the ordinary matter brain. Thus, contrary to the Christian credo, souls are not, according to the present theory, created in a divine act but codevelop gradually with ordinary matter human brains.

The present theory, of course, is not a religious view, but the view embraced by the author who is a mechanistic materialist. The present view that the soul during its development becomes structured by the ordinary matter brain acting as a template is important. As Prabhu (1989, p. 69) notes, the contrary doctrine of divine creation of the soul 'saddles God with the responsibility for inequalities [of souls].' Indeed, according to the orthodox (religious) doctrine one would have to assume that God creates the souls of good people and also of criminals and super-criminals like Hitler. I have also written elsewhere on some of the problematics of creationism (Wassermann, 1982, *Nature* (London) *296*, 284). As Prabhu aptly noted about the alleged divine creation of souls (l.c. p. 69) 'The implications of this ascription are at the very least problematical for a traditional conception of God as all-good and all-powerful.'

4.14 Properties of disembodied Souls
S.T. Davis (1989, p. 123) writes:

'Which properties typical of embodied human persons will disembodied souls have and which will they lack? Clearly they will lack those properties that essentially involve corporeality. They will possess no spatial location, for example at least not in the space-time manifold with which we are familiar. They will not be able to perceive their surroundings (using the spatial word surroundings in a stretched sense)—not at least in the ways in which we perceive our surroundings (that is through the eyes, ears, and so on). They will not be able to experience bodily pains and pleasures. They will not be able to engage in bodily activities. Taking a walk, getting dressed, playing catch—these sort of activities will be impossible.'

Seen from the point of view of my theory much, or most, of the preceding passage does not apply to the Shadow Matter body and its soul. Shadow Matter souls are (by hypothesis) material systems. Unlike the immaterial souls presumably envisaged by Davis, they may have (together with the rest of the disembodied Shadow Matter body) properties that essentially involve corporeality (namely corporeality of the Shadow Matter body, including its soul). By means of Shadow Matter eyes of the Shadow Matter body they will be able to see their surroundings (Wassermann, 1993). This, according to Wassermann (1993), is already inherent in out-of-the-body experiences (OBEs). In my theory it is assumed that in an OBE the Shadow Matter body and its soul become partly or almost completely detached from the ordinary matter body. Also the Shadow Matter eyes, jointly with the Shadow Matter brain (= soul) can see much of the outside of the perceiver's ordinary matter body.

More significantly, perhaps, is that the soul, according to my theory, is the repository of, often immensely subtle and complex memories, which can be recalled. Thus, a great mathematician such as Andrew Wiles could have stored in his soul the whole of his highly intricate famous proof of Fermat's celebrated last theorem. Accordingly, externalizing such a proof *via* the ordinary matter body with the aid of paper and pencil is only a minor aspect of a proof that in reality is stored in the soul (= Shadow Matter brain).

At death a perceiver's ordinary matter body could also be seen (before it disintegrates) from the outside by that perceiver. All this is consistent with what happens in OBEs of Near Death Experiences (NDEs). Also the normal perception of pain could be transacted partly with the help of Shadow Matter pain receptors (for which the ordinary matter pain receptors act only as a support system). If so then the detached Shadow Matter body could still perceive pain (see Section 4.6 for the assumed pain perceived in hell and its mechanisms). Pleasurable sensations (e.g. of the kinds we experience in coitus) could be enhanced by the much reduced pressure in the upper regions of the Shadow Matter ocean (in heaven) on Shadow Matter bodies (including their souls). I conclude that few of Davis' assumptions about disembodied *immaterial* souls (see earlier this section) need apply to disembodied Shadow Matter souls. I have also repeatedly stressed that (according to the present theory) the Shadow Matter soul is in life and death (i.e. in survival) the seat of mentality. (This includes *consciousness*, beliefs, wishes, knowledge, memory etc. (see Davis 1989 p. 124)). (Contrary to my theory which is based on assumed material souls (i.e. Shadow Matter souls) the late Oxford Professor H.H. Price (1978) in his article 'Survival and the Idea of 'Another World" in John Donnelly (ed.) *Language Metaphysics and Death* (New York, Fordham University Press pp. 176–95), cited by Davis (1989), assumes that souls are immaterial (cf. Wassermann, 1993, p. 166). However, if souls were immaterial then it is hard to see how, as Price (1978) claims, probably correctly, surviving souls could communicate telepathically, if telepathy is a physical process (as suggested by Wassermann, 1993).

5 Reincarnation and Survival

5.1 Introductory Remarks on Reincarnation

According to the present theory, as ordinary matter brains evolved so did their associated Shadow Matter brains (= souls). This, in turn, led to the evolution of consciousness, which is here regarded as a byproduct (epiphenomenon) of the soul. In addition, I postulated that at death souls survive and could migrate to Shadow Matter regions of the Earth (or associated with it) which are, possibly, similar to regions that are traditionally labelled as either heaven or hell, as appropriate.

There are a good many people living on this Earth who share beliefs differing from the hypotheses here propounded and just mentioned. Many of these people believe in repeated rebirths. According to them at death a particular soul of a particular individual may become associated with another (living) individual (a process that is similar to, or identical with, so-called reincarnation). The same soul, in turn, at death of its new owner, could migrate to, and become associated with, yet another owner, and so forth. *Repeated* rebirths (as distinct from a single resurfacing of a past personality in another person, i.e. reincarnation) are rare, and, perhaps a matter of religion rather than fact.

Cases of reincarnation are well established notably by the extensive studies of Professor Ian Stevenson, who is the world leader in this field. He has written many books on reincarnation, as well as numerous articles which are extremely valuable, even if one does not share all of his views on this large subject. I can in this book only discuss a few important aspects of this vast topic and leave readers who wish to explore Stevenson's studies in depth to turn to his important publications directly. I shall here only rely on a few extracts from Stevenson's (1987) book *Children who remember previous Lives*.

Although putative cases of reincarnation have been attempted to be explicable as cases of telepathy and other psiphenomena, I prefer to accept reincarnation explanations. I am, apart from my own studies of a variety of Stevenson's cases, reinforced in my belief by Stevenson's own verdict. He is cited by Prabhu (1989, p. 75) as having said in an interview in 1974

> *'what I do believe is that of the cases we now know, reincarnation—at least for some—is the best explanation that we have been able to come up with. There is an impressive body of evidence and it is getting stronger all the time. I think a rational person, if he wants, can believe in reincarnation on the the basis of evidence.'*

While I share this view fully, I realize that a fuller explanation of reincarnation requires also a theory of the mechanisms of reincarnation. In my earlier book on psi-phenomena (Wassermann, 1993) I did not discuss reincarnation phenomena, let alone their mechanisms, and this is the first time that I am doing so. However, let me stress that cases of reincarnation of the kind studied by Stevenson, though numerous, show only that in some cases a person, usually a child, may exhibit memories or other cognitive traits that were typical for someone. That 'someone' lived before that child and was unknown to that child. But such cases do not give license to make (on their basis) claims for supposed repeated rebirths, in which allegedly the same soul turned up serially in a sequence of people who lived in serial order. Granted that logically such cases are conceivable, to the best of my knowledge such claims can only be a matter of religion but have no reliable empirical foundation (as distinct from reincarnation cases).

For instance, Glucklich (1989, p. 82) cites the sort of phenomenon, which I do not think has a scientific basis. He writes 'The Sakyamuni Buddha emerged out of his mother's womb after having undergone an enormous number of previous rebirths'. While any Buddhist may believe this, it is not a matter of empirical knowledge (at least as far as I am aware). Such religious claims of Buddhism (etc.)

are certainly not related to the type of evidence for reincarnation studied by Stevenson and others. Indeed consider the case of a supposedly repeatedly reborn goat cited by Glucklich (l.c. p. 83). Glucklich cites that the goat was brought before a Brahmin and

> 'when brought before the Brahmin the goat explained: I too was a Brahmin who sacrificed a goat on behalf of my ancestors. As a result I have been damned to live hundred births as a goat, each life terminating with a sacrificial beheading. This is my 500th birth and today I will finally be able to terminate this suffering and return to a human existence.'

Apart from the circumstance that we have here a goat that can talk in human language, a state of affairs usually confined to children's stories, this goat had, apparently human genes for cognitive procedures in a body otherwise controlled by genes of a biological goat. I do not think that this kind of rebirth fairy tale can appeal to any right-minded biologist except as a fairy tale. It certainly does not make repeated rebirth the least bit likely. I am writing all this, redundant as it may seem, to avoid any possible confusion of this and reincarnation, as studied by Professor Ian Stevenson. A confusion of the religious notion of rebirth (inherent in some Eastern religions) with reincarnation as studied by Stevenson may not be uncommon.

Thus, Glucklich (1989, p. 86) writes, towards the end of his paper. 'We may be highly impressed by the evidence which Ian Stevenson marshals in support of rebirth, but we cannot ground the conceptual framework for his and other's hypotheses on the Indian doctrines of *karma* and rebirth (Stevenson, 1966).' Here we see the clear danger in Glucklich's cited passage of calling both the Indian doctrine of rebirth and Stevenson's phenomena 'rebirth'. This, muddle of course does not appear in Stevenson's work. He wisely refers to the phenomena studied by him as *reincarnation*. These scientific studies cannot be used to lend support to religious doctrines, particularly when these claim repeated rebirth of the same personality. Nor do such religious claims in any way reinforce the validity of Professor Stevenson's important findings.

5.2 Class Characteristics of Reincarnation Phenomena

In this section I shall try to provide a quasi-synoptic heavily condensed account of Ian Stevenson's (1987) book, so as to give readers some idea what reincarnation phenomena refer to and some of their principal properties. In the following section I shall try to provide a Shadow Matter theory of reincarnation phenomena, thereby trying to bring these phenomena into line with my general theory.

Stevenson's (1987) book is 'about children who claim to remember previous lives' (1987, p. 1). These previous lives were not in those children's body but in the bodies of other persons e.g. typically grown up people. The number of cases investigated exceeds 2000 (1987, p. 1). Probably only a relatively small fraction of the human population of this planet display verifiable reincarnation phenomena. The reincarnated personality is supposed to have survived the death of a previous body that it inhabited. Stevenson (1987, p. 3) seems to believe that in a reincarnation case there occurs an association of a discarnate personality with a new physical body. By contrast I assume that in a reincarnation there occurs the detachment of a Shadow Matter brain (= soul) of a newly or recently deceased person. The detached (surviving) soul can then move about in 3-D space and, by trial and error, try to associate with the Shadow Matter brains of one or more living people.

If the searching soul does not fit any particular living soul, then it moves on. If, however, the searching soul achieves a sufficiently close fit of a living soul then it becomes physically strongly or weakly bonded to that living soul, the strength of bonding depending on the degree of similarity (perhaps mainly genetical) of the searching soul and the soul to which it binds. Thus the assumed 'association' is in my theory not between a discarnate 'personality' and a new physical body, but between a released soul and an existing soul bound to a living body. Granted, the released soul of the dead body is surviving and, thus, the carrier of a discarnate personality. When the released soul binds to the soul of a recipient person then, in appropriate circumstances, it could act on the ordinary matter brain of the recipient person and, thereby communicate, via the recipient person's communication system information associated with the released soul (= Shadow Matter brain).

Stevenson argues, I think correctly, that 'the association of a discarnate personality with a new physical body would entail major adaptations as it becomes housed in a new and smaller physical frame [of a child] with still rudimentary sensory organs.' (1987 p. 3) In terms of my theory this would mean that the released soul could be much larger than the soul of the recipient. However, this presents no problem.

I postulated already in Wassermann (1993) in different contexts that *Shadow Matter is a highly elastic substance.* Accordingly, as the released soul tries to adapt to the recipient soul the released soul could shrink, and/or the recipient soul could expand, thereby allowing an adequate fit between the two souls. Thus, I do not have to invoke any new hypotheses, but can fall back on several of my earlier hypotheses of Wassermann (1993). Elastic deformations of the released Shadow Matter body (and its released soul) could also be instrumental in some of the other adaptations to which Stevenson (1987, pp. 3–4) refers.

Stevenson (1987) states that:

'The evidence for reincarnation that we have suggests that living human beings (and perhaps non-human animals also) have minds, or souls if you like, that animate them when they are living and that survive after they die.'

I have, independently of Stevenson, reached similar conclusions, as regards the existence of souls (= Shadow Matter brains not discussed by Stevenson) in Wassermann (1993) and throughout the preceding chapters of this book. This is not vitalism, since the soul postulated here is a material entity composed of Shadow Matter. Shadow Matter was first postulated by Kolb *et al* (1985) in the respectable journal *Nature* (London). Any scientist who proclaims that *a priori* Shadow Matter could not exist is possibly as justified in his or her claims as those many virulently prejudiced people who claimed, last century, that hypnotism could not exist. Indeed, as far as I can see, there is nothing in orthodox science that contradicts my theory of Wassermann (1993) and earlier arguments presented in this book. Stevenson published his (1987) book one year before I first presented my then new Shadow Matter theory of psychic phenomena in the prominent journal *Inquiry* (Wassermann, 1988) in its earlier form. Hence, my present interpretations were not possible when Stevenson published his book.

In case anyone should ask how a Shadow Matter brain (= soul) could leave or enter a skull, let me remind them that earlier in this book (and in Wassermann 1993) I noted that Shadow matter can, apparently without resistance, penetrate through ordinary matter (and vice versa).

(At this point let me interpose some cautionary remarks. In his (1987) book Stevenson also relates several fascinating spontaneous case accounts of apparent precognitive and/or clairvoyant cases. In most of these cases corroborative statements by independent witnesses exist. In my own accounts of spontaneous case histories I have (Wassermann, 1993) usually abstained from giving existing corroborative accounts, on the assumption that skeptics could look these up in the sources cited. My aim was, rather, to provide novel materialistic mechanistic explanations of the cases cited, rather than have endless debates with skeptics who no amount of corroboration could satisfy. Such hyperskeptics will, with mounting positive case histories be shown to have been not only unfair but stupid into the bargain.

For instance one person with a Ph.D. bluntly denied that out-of-the-body experiences (OBEs) despite massive evidence from cases of Near Death experiences (NDEs) do exist! It is a waste of time to argue with such people who are excessively dogmatic. Until recently one of the cardinal weaknesses of both spontaneous cases and experimental findings in parapsychology was the absence of a comprehensive explanatory theory that could 'make sense' of such phenomena and findings.

In order to overcome this shortcoming I developed and published a comprehensive theory of paranormal phenomena (Wassermann, 1993, 1988). This is driven further in this book. Particularly in order to deal with reincarnation phenomena, see above in this section and elsewhere in this chapter. There are many cases where the phenomena that occurred had quite typical *class characteristics* (reincarnation phenomena are typical examples) and in such cases we can safely rule out 'chance coincidences' and similar nonsense relied on by pathological hypercritics.

After this lengthy side-tracking let me return to the main topic of this chapter, namely reincarnation and its possible mechanisms and class characteristics. In Chapter 11 of his (1987) book Stevenson has made some suggestions concerning possible processes that may be involved in reincarnation. He asks (l.c. p. 237):

'If reincarnation occurs what reincarnates? Why is a person born in one

family instead of in some other one? How can a discarnate personality who is about to reincarnate influence the physical body of the next incarnation? Does conduct in one life influence the circumstances of another one?'

Instead of simply repeating how Stevenson answered these questions let me answer these questions in terms of my preceding theory, given at the start of this section.

5.3 Further Discussion of the likely Mechanisms of Reincarnation

Near the start of Section 5.2 I postulated a novel mechanism of reincarnation. It was suggested that at death the Shadow Matter brain of the deceased person becomes detached from the ordinary matter brain of that person. The detached Shadow Matter brain could then make random walks in space and attempt to fit the Shadow Matter brains of other (living) people, until a suitable match is made between the migrating Shadow Matter brain and the Shadow Matter brain of a living person.

When this occurs a strong bond is established between the (no longer) migrating Shadow Matter brain of the dead person and the Shadow Matter brain of the living person (the recipient). This answers at once Stevenson's first question 'what reincarnates?' The answer given in my theory is that what reincarnates is the detached, random-walking Shadow Matter brain of the deceased person. It is evident that the capture by a matching brain is a relatively rare process. The surviving Shadow Matter brain of the deceased person is the carrier of all that person's intellectual facilities, including his memories and cognitive facilities. It follows that the captured Shadow Matter brain can make use of the somatic machinery of the capturing host in much the same way as the host's own Shadow Matter brain can make use of that somatic machinery.

This also answer's Stevenson's third question 'how can a discarnate personality who is about to reincarnate influence the physical body of the next incarnation?' First, what reincarnates is primarily the migrating Shadow Matter brain of the deceased person. That Shadow Matter brain is also the carrier of that dead person's personality (it was so during the life of that person and is assumed to remain so after death). It follows that the personality of the dead person migrates with his Shadow Matter brain until that Shadow Matter brain becomes anchored to a matching recipient brain. In this way the personality of the dead person forms an additional personality of the living recipient. What influences the physical body of the recipient host body is, however, not the personality of the deceased person, but the captured Shadow Matter brain of the deceased person.

Next, Professor Stevenson asks 'Does conduct in one life influence the circumstances of another one?' My answer to this question is strongly affirmative, because of the explanatory mechanism I have propounded. Let me explain. According to my theory conduct of a living person is dictated by the Shadow Matter brain, combined with the ordinary matter brain of that person and the rest of his or her body. This conduct may also leave memory traces, i.e. engrams on that person's Shadow Matter brain.

When that person dies and his or her Shadow Matter brain migrates the surviving engrams of past conduct (in the earlier life) move with the surviving migrating Shadow Matter brain. When the latter becomes captured by the matching Shadow Matter brain of a recipient host person, the engrams of the captured Shadow Matter brain could interact with the ordinary matter brain of the host and influence his or her circumstances. (It must be stressed that according to my theory engrams are carried (like all other mentality representing structures) by the Shadow Matter brain and *not* by the ordinary matter brain.)

Stevenson also asks 'Why is a person born in one family instead of in some other one?' The obvious answer would seem to be 'because that person's parents were the ones who had sexual intercourse.' But this is, perhaps, not quite the answer which Professor Stevenson had in mind.

Of course, according to my theory, only a few Shadow Matter brains (= souls) reincarnate, the vast majority, at death, migrate either to heaven or to hell.

How does this, newly proposed, machinery of reincarnation manifest itself in actual case histories? To fathom this one must study Stevenson's important pioneering books on the subject. I shall here only give a few snippets, a few extracts from Stevenson's (1987) book, to whet the reader's appetite for digging further into Stevenson's vast numbers of contributions. Thus in his (1987, p. 238) Stevenson states:

'For example, a boy who claims he has a wife and children in another village wants to go and see them; another boy who remembers the life of a doctor likes to play at being a doctor; and a third who describes being shot to death points to a birthmark that he says derives from the shooting and expresses an intention of taking revenge on the murderer.'

Thus, the reincarnated Shadow Matter brain can still cogitate autonomously about past affairs. *Birthmarks* of the kind described could be due to psychokineses exerted by the reincarnated Shadow Matter brain on the living body within which it resides.

Stevenson postulates a 'vehicle that carries a person's mental elements between incarnations' and calls it a *psychophore*. In my theory there is no need to postulate such a special carrier, since the Shadow Matter brain of the deceased person moves in space and acts as a carrier of the deceased person's surviving mentality. Whereas Professor Stevenson (1987 p. 239) is uncertain whether a personality can reincarnate entirely (since there is no evidence for this), my theory is consistent with the possibility of reincarnation of an entire personality. The Shadow Matter brain (= soul) of a deceased person carries the complete personality of that person, according to my theory. This, however, does not mean that that entire personality (rather than a fraction of it) can be expressed by the recipient host. (Personality, as discussed here may be something more like mentality.)

The manner in which a surviving soul of a dead person is being 'piloted' to the living Shadow Matter brain of a matching recipient could depend on telepathy. I have already postulated at length how the mechanism of telepathy could operate in terms of my Shadow Matter theory (see Wassermann, 1993). In contrast to this Stevenson seems to rely on emotional factors as piloting 'factors'. For instance he suggests (l.c. p. 241) that 'animosities . . . seem to bind'.

I am reluctant to invoke such, and other, semi-animistic piloting 'factors' and prefer my mechanistic theory, unless in years to come overwhelming evidence of such 'non-mechanistic factors' becomes apparent. For instance Stevenson (1987, p. 242) argues that 'a devout Buddhist who believes that he must pay for everything—now or later—could die with a burden on his conscience that might bind him to the creditor and lead to rebirth in the creditor's family.'

I am reluctant to accept such an interpretation unless numerous other cases call for, or are consistent with, interpretations of the same type. The tendency of some interpreters of such cases to postulate a 'binding' or attraction between the souls of living and dead people (cf. Stevenson, l.c. p. 242) rather than physically mediated processes also do not appeal to me. I would only invoke these if a large number of cases compelled me to do so, which is not the case. Indeed Stevenson (1987, p. 242) himself states that he 'should acknowledge immediately that for the majority of long-distance cases [he has] no clues whatever as to why the subject was born in his family.' I still believe that random encounters (as postulated above) or in some cases telepathy could provide suitable explanatory factors why a particular Shadow Matter brain of a deceased person could turn up in a child of a particular family.

5.4 A very few Case Histories of Reincarnations

To get the flavour of case histories of reincarnations one must refer to Stevenson's massive published material (cf. Stevenson, 1987 for relatively few such cases). With the kind permission of Professor Stevenson I shall cite two cases from Professor Stevenson. This is a tiny sample. In fact, this does not matter since, for many purposes, one case of reincarnation is much like the next. Let me here just cite two cases. One of these comes from Stevenson (1987, p. 244). Stevenson writes:

> 'In several cases the subject [of a reincarnation experience] was born at a place to which the previous personality's body had been carried after his death. A subject in Burma, Maung Aye Kyaw, remembered that he had been shot in the previous life and his body had been thrown into a small river. Maung Aye Kyaw recalled that in his discarnate state he had followed the body as it drifted downstream. Some miles below the place of the murder, the floating cadaver became stuck against the pilings of a small dock near a house on the bank of the river. A woman of the house noticed the body in the water and called some men, who pushed it back into the stream, causing it to be carried farther down the streams to the Irrawaddy River,

soon afterward the woman became pregnant with Maung Aye Kyaw, who, when he could speak narrated these details.' There is every reason to believe that Stevenson, as in massive numbers of other cases, carefully checked up on the case history.

Next I have choosen a case from Stevenson's (1987) Chapter 4, which is headed 'Twelve Typical Cases of Children who remember previous Lives'. The case choosen that of Suleyman Andary is very long, and displays the thoroughness typical of almost all of Stevenson's massive numbers of investigations. Stevenson (1987, p. 64) writes

'Suleyman Andary was born in Falougha, Lebanon, on March 4, 1954. His family were Druses, members of a religion that derived from Islam. This religion has, however, separated so much from orthodox Islamic teachings that its members now regard it as separate. Reincarnation is a central tenet of the Druse religion.'

'As a young child, Suleyman seemed to remember fragmentarily a few details of a previous life. Some of the information came to him in dreams. He recalled having had children and knew some of their names, and he remembered that he was from a place called Gharife and had owned an oil press there. Unlike most children subjects of these cases, however, he did not recall additional details until he was considerably older.'

'When he was about eleven, a particular episode appears to have stimulated further memories. He was living then with his paternal grandmother. His maternal grandmother came to the house and asked to borrow one of the Druse religious books. Suleyman refused her request rather curtly, asking her whether she did not have the book at her home. (He apparently did not stop to think that if she had had the book, she would not have come to borrow it.) His paternal grandmother overheard his rude handling of his other grandmother and asked him to explain his conduct. Suddenly, he remembered that he had had religious books in a previous life and that he had not allowed them to leave the house. Druses who have copies of their

religious books almost venerate them and preserve them carefully at home; Suleyman's attitude, therefore, although impolite for a young boy, accorded well with what one might expect of an older Druse man.'

'After this incident, Suleyman made a more or less deliberate effort to retrieve further details of the previous life he seemed to be remembering. He then recalled that he had been the mukhtar (headman) of Gharife. He also remembered the mukhtar's name, Abdallah Abu Hamdan, and other details of his life. Now, however, Suleyman became afraid of being teased if he told people that he had been a mukhtar in a previous life. His family and friends, he thought, would accuse him of arrogance or would deride him. So he kept his memories to himself for almost another two years. He then talked a little about them, at first with other children and later with adults.'

'Some of Suleyman's adult relatives proposed to take him to Gharife in order to verify what he was saying about a previous life there. Gharife is about 30 kilometers from Falougha, but in a different region of Lebanon. Although roads connect the two villages, it takes some effort and a special reason to travel from one to the other, as I found myself. With one exception, members of Suleyman's family had no connections with Gharife. One member was employed there temporarily, but he could not confirm from his own knowledge what Suleyman was saying about a previous life in Gharife. Later, this relative made inquiries in Gharife and managed to verify a few of Suleyman's statements. In the meantime, other persons had also confirmed the accuracy of some of these statements.'

'As usually happens in these cases in Asia, word about Suleyman's claims concerning a previous life spread to other persons. A cousin of his family met (in Saudi Arabia) some residents of Gharife and told them about Suleyman's statements. They confirmed that Suleyman's memories accorded with facts in the life of one Abdallah Abu Hamdan, who had owned an oil press and had been mukhtar of Gharife for many years before his death—probably of heart disease—in 1942 at the age of about sixty

Consciousness & Near Death Experiences 155

five. The Gharife residents who gave this information invited Suleyman to visit them. At first he refused, but then in the late summer and autumn of 1967 he went twice to Gharife.'

'Suleyman seemed shy and inhibited in Gharife. Abdallah Abu Hamdan's widow and two of his children were still living there, but Suleyman did not recognize them, nor did he recognize members of the family in photographs. He did, however, recognize three other persons and a few places at Gharife. Perhaps the most important of these recognitions occurred when he pointed out an old road, no longer used and almost obliterated by 1967, for reaching the house where Abdallah Abu Hamdan had lived. However, the importance of Suleyman's case does not lie in his few recognitions. It derives instead from his statements about the previous life and from some unusual related behaviour that he showed.'

'Before going to Gharife, or during his first visit there, Suleyman made seventeen statements about the previous life. These included the names of most of Abdallah Abu Hamdan's children and some other details of his life. His statements were all correct with two exceptions: he gave the name of Salim as that of one of Abdallah Abu Hamdan's sons, whereas Salim was his brother; and he said that Salim was blind, whereas a son of Abdallah Abu Hamdan named Naseeb was blind, but Salim was not.'

Stevenson continues his account of this case thus:

'I began investigating this case in March 1968 and continued working on it until 1972. I interviewed numerous informants in Falougha and Gharife. Suleyman later emigrated to Saudi Arabia, and I have not met him since 1972.'

'When he was still a young child, Suleyman comported himself like an adult. He preferred the company of adults to that of children, and even in a group of adults he tended to seat himself prominently among them as an important person might do. He objected if anyone scolded him, and when this happened he would say something like: 'One does not scold me. I am an adult.'

'Suleyman's fears that other persons would laugh at him if they knew he claimed to have been a mukhtar in a previous life proved sound, his family and friends did tease him for his pretensions, and they even nicknamed him 'Mukhtar'. This did not altogether displease him, especially as some members of the family seemed to use the nickname affectionately, as if to say: 'We believe you.' And indeed they did believe him after they had verified his statements about the life of Abdallah Abu Hamdan.'

'Suleyman also showed greater concern about religion than the other members of his family did. This accorded with Abdallah Abu Hamdan's strong interest in religion: toward the end of his life, he had become a sheikh, which meant taking vows to maintain a much higher standard of conduct than ordinary people aspire to.'

Professor Stevenson continues:

'I mentioned earlier that Suleyman did not wish to visit Gharife, and when he was first invited to do so, he refused. His family understood this better when, at Gharife, they learned of the tragedies in the life of Abdallah Abu Hamdan. Abdallah Abu Hamdan's children had given him little comfort; several had congenital deformities, one had emigrated to America, and another had a poor relationship with his father. Then other events darkened the last days of his life. In order to help a friend, Abdallah Abu Hamdan had foolishly falsified a document that, as mukhtar of his village, he had to execute; when the government learned of his deception, he was dismissed from his office as mukhtar. Finally, he invested beyond his means in an oil press. The payments for this proved more burdensome than he had expected, and, according to his wife, worry about his indebtedness brought on his final illness. No one could feel surprised, therefore, that anyone claiming to have Abdallah Abu Hamdan's memories would not rush over to Gharife.'

Stevenson continues further:

> 'As I mentioned, Abdallah Abu Hamdan died in 1942, twelve years before Suleyman's birth. If Abdallah Abu Hamdan had reincarnated as Suleyman, where had he spent the interval? Suleyman answered this question saying that he had an intermediate life of which he remembered nothing. This is the stock answer of Druses when an interval—even of so little as a single day—occurs between the death of an identified previous personality in a case and the subject's birth. Occasionally one may find some slender evidence of such intermediate lives, but usually they remain entirely conjectural.'

[*Note by the present author*. According to my theory of reincarnation (Section 5.2 and Section 5.3) it was assumed that the Shadow Matter brain (= soul) of a deceased person can roam about in space until it finds a matching brain of a suitable subject. This period of roaming about could account for the temporal interval between death of one person and the reincarnation of his or her soul by another person.]

Now, let me return to the last paragraph of Professor Stevenson's account of the present case.

> 'With regard to Suleyman's memories of the life of Abdallah Abu Hamdan, however, I do not think they derived from information he obtained through ordinary means of communication. The distance between the villages concerned in this case—30 kilometers—considerably exceeded that in Shamlinie Prema's case, although it was much less than that in Gopal Gupta's. Yet we should not measure accessibility only in kilometers. We must evaluate all the possibilities by which a subject could have obtained normally the information he had about the previous personality. Assessing it in this way I am inclined to rank Suleyman's case above that of Shamlinie, in which the two families concerned had some slight acquaintance before her case developed. It is perhaps on the same level of Gopal's case. In the latter case there were greater geographical and socioeconomic separations between the families concerned than in

Suleyman's case; but Gopal was remembering the life of a prominent man whose murder by his brother became a sensation, whereas Suleyman's memories related to a person about whose life and death little information had diffused outside his village.'

5.5 Additional Comments on the Findings of Stevenson

In (Stevenson, 1987, p. 54) Stevenson explains why he values 'so highly the spontaneous utterances about previous lives made by young children' and why, almost exclusively young children formed the subjects of his reincarnation studies. One main reason why adults prove to be less suitable subjects for reincarnation studies seems to be the overcrowding of their mentality storing and receiving systems with existing memories, which makes these people less accessible to be subjects of reincarnation.

Among the class characteristics of reincarnation cases that Stevenson mentions (1987, p. 97) is the finding that the child (who is the subject of the reincarnation) 'behaves in ways that are unusual in his family but that informants say match behaviour that the deceased person had shown or that might have been expected of him.' This, again, is consistent with my theory of reincarnation given above. The reincarnating Shadow Matter brain (=soul) of the deceased person has stored the typical behaviour patterns of that person and, when the reincarnated soul controls (temporarily) behaviour then that behaviour could be expected to correspond to that of the deceased person rather than that typical of the family to which the child belongs.

Interestingly Stevenson (1987, p. 107) states that:

> 'The child's memories tend to cluster around events of the last year, month, and days of the life [of the deceased person] remembered. Nearly three-quarters of the subjects claim to remember how the person of the previous life died, and they remember this detail more often when the death was violent than when it occurred naturally.' According to my theory Shadow Matter brains (= souls) in life and after death are capable of serially ordered memory recall. We know this, for instance (by conjecture) from the ability of a concert pianist to play a complete sonata off by heart.

Similarly, a soul of a deceased person that has become transferred to the reincarnating subject could, in serial order recall the events of the terminal stages of the deceased person from whom that soul derives. Likewise, by transfer with the reincarnating Shadow Matter brain, the machinery for recognition of formerly known, 'familiar' people or sights (etc.) becomes transferred to the subject of the reincarnation. The transferred Shadow Matter brain (= soul) could make use, in recognitions, of the subject's Shadow Matter eyes and Shadow Matter nervous system.

5.6 *Coda*

I have now come to the end of this relatively short, but far-reaching book. Together with my earlier book *Shadow Matter And Psychic Phenomena* (Oxford Mandrake, 1993) it presents a coherent and comprehensive theory of psychic phenomena. This theory is fully mechanistic and materialistic. It links up with contemporary sciences, so that psi-phenomena no longer remain isolated bits which we cannot explain. This is the case in most or all previous theories of paranormal phenomena. The final chapter of this book owes much to the writings of Professor Ian Stevenson, although the theorizing is novel.

Many people have misguidedly thought that the real value of parapsychology lies allegedly in its supposed capacity to demonstrate that mechanistic materialism is a bankrupt doctrine. Far from this being the case, the present theory in this book and in Wassermann (1993) may help to demonstrate once and for all that mechanistic materialism is a valid doctrine, into which a theory of paranormal phenomena, like the present one, may be incorporated, and which might bring intellectual satisfaction to many people.

Bibliography

Bem, Daryl J. and Honorton, Charles (1994) 'Does Psi Exist? Replicable Evidence for an Anomalous Process of Information Transfer' *Psychological Bulletin 115* no. 1, 4–18

Blackmore, S. (1982) *Beyond the Body* (London, Heinemann)

Blackmore, S. (1986) *The Adventures of a Parapsychologist* (Buffalo, New York, Prometheus)

Blackmore, S. (1993) *Dying to Live* (London, Harper Collins Publishers)

Bowker, J. (1991) *The Meanings of Death* (Cambridge, Cambridge University Press)

Brain (Lord) W.R. (1951) *Mind Perception and Science* (Oxford, Blackwell)

Broughton, R. ((1991) *Parapsychology* The controversial Science (London, Rider)

Byerly, T.C. and Olsen, M.W. (1934) *Science*, 80, 247

Cartlidge (1991) cited by Fenwick (1996)

Chalmers (1995) cited by Clarke (1995)

Clarke, C.J.S. (1995) 'The Nonlocality of Mind' *Journal of Consciousness Studies* *2* no. 3, pp. 231–240

Clowes, J. and Wassermann, G.D. (1984) *Bulletin of Mathematical Biology 46*, 785–825

Cook, N.D. (1977) 'The Case for Reverse Translation' *Journal of Theoretical Biology* 64, 113-135

Cottingham (1992) cited by Clarke (1995)

Cowan, J.D. (1982) Spontaneous Symmetry breaking in large-scale nervous activity, *International Journal of Quantum Chemistry 22*, 1054–82

Davenport, C.B. (1920) *Proc. Soc. Exp. Biol. and Med.* 17, 75

Davis, S.T. (1989) (ed.) *Death and Afterlife* (London, Macmillan)

Davis, S.T. (1989) 'The Resurrection of the Dead' in S.T. Davis (ed.) (1989) *Death and Afterlife* (London, Macmillan) Chapter 5

Drab, K. (1981) 'The tunnel experience' Reality or Hallucination?' *Anabiosis: The Journal of Near-Death Studies*, 1, 126–52

Fenwick, E. and Fenwick, P. (1995) *The Truth in the Light* (Hoddor, Headline)

Fenwick, P. (1991) Progress in IANDS research, *IANDS News Bulletin* (UK) Autumn 1991

Fenwick, P. (1994) Review of *Dying to Live* by Susan Blackmore (The Scientific and Medical Network Newsletter no. 55, 74 (Editor David Lorimer, Gibliston Mill, Colinsburgh, Leven, Fife Scotland KY9 IJS)

Fenwick, P. (1996) *Journal of Near Death Experiences*

Flew, A. (1967) 'Immortality' in P. Edwards (ed.) *The Encyclopaedia of Philosophy* (New York, Macmillan)

Flew, A. (1976) *The Presumption of Atheism and other Essays* (London, Elek/Pemberton)

Fodor, J.A. (1968) *Psychological Explanations: An Introduction of the Philosophy of Psychology* (New York, Random House)

Gabbard, G.O., Twemlow, S.W. and Jones, F.C. (1981) 'Do "near-death experiences" only occur near death?' *Journal of Nervous and Mental Disease* 169, 174-197

Geach, P.T. (1969) *God and the Soul* (London Routledge and Kegan Paul)

Gillett, G.R. (1986) 'Disembodied Persons' *Philosophy 61*, pp. 377–86

Glucklich, A. (1989) Karma and Rebirth in India, in S.T. Davis (ed.) (1989) *Death and Afterlife* (London, Macmillan pp. 81–87)

Green, C. (1976) *The Decline and Fall of Science* (London, Hamish Hamilton)

Green, M.B. (1985) Unification of Forces and Particles in Superstring Theories *Nature*, (London) *314*, 409–414

Grinspoon, L. and Bakalar, J. (1979) *Psychedelic Drugs Reconsidered* (New York, Basic Books)

Helm, P. (1978) 'A Theory of Disembodied Survival and Re-embodied Existence' *Religious Studies 14* (1)

Hick, J. (1989) 'A possible Conception of Life after Death' in S.T. Davis (ed.) (1989) *Death and Afterlife* (London Macmillan) pp. 183 ff

Huxley, J. (1942) *Evolution, The Modern Synthesis*

Hyslop, J.H. (1901) 'A further record of Observations of Certain Trance Phenomena', Proc. S.P.R. *16* (41) p. 291

Irish, J.A. (1989) 'From Here to Eternity: A Response to Davis' in *Death and Afterlife* S.T. Davis (ed.) (1989) (London, Macmillan) pp. 183 ff

Irwin, H.J. (1985) *Height of Mind: A psychological Study of the out-of-body Experience*, (Metuchen, New Jersey, Scarecrow Press)

Jacobson, M. (1969) 'Development of specific neuronal connections' *Science* 163, 543-547

Jansen, R.I. (1996) cited by Fenwick (1996)

Köhler, W. (1940) *Dynamics in Psychology* (New York, Liveright)

Kolb, E.W., Seckel, D. & Turner, M.S. (1985) 'The Shadow World of Superstring Theories', *Nature* (London) *314*, 415–419

Lashley, K.S. (1950) 'In Search of the Engram' in *Physiological Mechanisms In Animal Behaviour Symposia of the society of Experimental Biology* (Cambridge, Cambridge University Press)

Lashley, K.S. (1950) 'In Search of the Engram' in Symposia of the Society of Experimental Biology no. 4 *Physiological Mechanisms in Animal Behaviour* p. 454

Lashley, K.S. (1951) 'The Problem of Serial Order in Behavior' in L. Jeffress (ed. *Cerebral Mechanisms in Behaviour* pp. 112ff (New York, John Wiley and Sons)

Lazarus, R. (1993) *The Case Against Death* (London, Warner Books, A Division of Little Brown & Co (UK))

Lenneberg, E.H. (1970) in *The Neurosciences, Second Study Program*

Lyon, A. (1988) in *An Encyclopaedia of Philosophy* (G.H.R. Parkinson ed.) London, Routledge 441

Mackie, J.L. (1985) *Persons and Values* (Oxford, Clarendon Press) pp. 1–27

Maddox, J. (1981) 'A Book fit for burning' *Nature*, (London) *293*, 245–246

Meduna L.J. (1950) 'The Effect of Carbon Dioxide Therapy upon Functionings of the Brain' in *Carbon Dioxide Therapy* (Springfield, Illinois, Charles C. Thomas)

Mekler, L.B. (1967) 'Mechanisms of Biological Memory' *Nature* (London) 215, 481-484

Moody, R.A. (1976) *Life after Life* (New York, Bantam Books)

Myers, F.W.H. (1892) 'On Indications of continued terenne knowledge on the part of phantasms of the Dead' *Proceedings of the Society for Psychical Research*

(London) *8*, 170–252

Needham, J. (1942) *Biochemistry and Morphogenisis* (Cambridge, Cambridge University Press)

Neisser, U. (1967) *Cognitive Psychology* (New York, Appleton)

Owens, J.E., Cook, E.W. and Stevenson, L. (1990) 'Features of "near-death experience" in relation to whether or not patients were near death' *The Lancet* 336, 1175-1177

Palay, S.L. (1967) *The Neurosciences* (F.O. Schmidt ed.) First Study Program (New York, Rockefeller University Press 1, 24)

Penelhum, T. (1970) *Survival and Disembodied Existence* (New York, Humanities Press)

Penelhum, T. (1982) 'Survival and Identity' in Mostafa Faghoury (ed.) *Analytical Philosophy of Religion in Canada* (Ottawa, Ontario, University of Ottawa Press)

Perry, J. (1978) *A Dialogue on Personal Identity and Immortality* (Indianapolis, Indiana, Hackett)

Phillips, D.Z. (1970) *Death and Immortality* (New York, St. Martin's Press)

Popper, K.R. and Eccles, J.C. (1977) *The Self and its Brain* (New York, Springer International)

Probhu, J. (1989) 'The Idea of Reincarnation' in S.T. Davis (ed.) (1989) *Death and Afterlife* (London, Macmillan) Chapter 3

Purtill, R.L. (1976) 'The Intelligibility of Disembodied Survival' *Christian Scholar's Review 5* (1)

Radin, D. (1997) *The Conscious Universe* (San Francisco, Harper Edge)

Redhead, M. (1987) *Incompleteness Nonlocality and Realism*: A Prolegomenon to the Philosophy of Quantum Mechanics (Oxford, Clarendon Press)

Reichenbach, B. (1983) *Is Man the Phoenix? A Study of Mortality* (Washington,

D.C. University Press of America)

Ring, K. (1982) p.216 cited by S. Blackmore (1993) p.260

Rogo, D.S. (1984) Keramine and the near death experience, *Anabiosis*—The Journal for Near-Death Studies *4*, 87–96

Semon, R. (1913) *Die Fuszsohle des Menschen, Arch. Mikr. Anat, 82* 164 (see also in Waddington (1957))

Sheldrake, R.A. (1981) *A New Science of Life* (London, Blond and Briggs)

Stevenson, I. (1966) *Twenty Cases suggestive of Reincarnation* (New York, American Society for Psychical Research)

Stevenson, I. (1987) *Children who remember previous Live*, A Question of Reincarnation (Charlottesville, University Press of Virginia)

Teasdale (1991) in Fenwick (1996)

Vernon, M.D. (1952) *A further Study of Visual Perception* (Cambridge, Cambridge University Press)

Waddington, C.H. (1957) *The Strategy of Genes,* (London, George Allen and Unwin)

Wassermann, G.D. (1972) *Molecular Control of Cell Differentiation and Morphogenesis* (New York, Marcel Dekker)

Wassermann, G.D. (1974) *Brains and Reasoning* (London, Macmillan)

Wassermann, G.D. (1978) *Neurobiological Theory of Psychological Phenomena* (London, Macmillan)

Wassermann, G.D. (1979) 'Reply to Popper's Attack on Epiphenomenalism' *Mind, 88*, 572–575

Wassermann, G.D. (1982a) 'TIMA Part 1. TIMA as a Paradigm for the Evolution of Molecular Complementarities' *Journal of Theoretical Biology*, 99, 77-86

Wassermann, G.D. (1982b) 'TIMA Part 2. TIMA-based Instructive Evolution of Macromolecules and Organs and Structures' *Journal of Theoretical Biology, 99,* 609-628

Wassermann, G.D. (1988) On a physical (materialistic) Theory of Psi-phenomena Based on Shadow Matter, *Inquiry 31,* 217–22

Wassermann, G.D. (1989) 'Theories, Systemic Models (SYMOs), Laws and Facts in the Sciences', *Synthese* 79, 489-514

Wassermann, G.D. (1993) *Shadow Matter and Psychic Phenomena* (Oxford, Mandrake of Oxford)

Wassermann, G.D. (1994) *A Philosophy of Matter and Mind* (Aldershot, Ashgate)

Wassermann, G.D. (1997) *Keys to Life* (Aldershot, Ashgate)

Wassermann, G.D. (1999) 'TIMA a recent Evolutionary Paradigm' In Solomon, P. Wasser (ed.) *Evolutionary Theory and Processes:* Modern Perspectives (Klüwer)

Wood-Jones, F. (1939) in Huxley (1942)

Wood-Jones, F. (1953) *Trends of Life* (London, Arnold)

Author Index

Aquinas, T *129*
Athenagoros *129*
Ayer, A J *131*
Bach, J S *126*
Bardeen *49, 109*
Beaufort, Sir Francis *95*
Bem, I and Honorton, C *36*
Blackmore, S *9, 10, 16, 17, 18, 19, 20, 21, 25, 26, 27, 28, 29, 30, 33, 34, 35, 36, 37, 38, 40, 43, 83, 84, 85, 86, 87, 89, 90, 91, 93, 94, 95, 96, 99, 102, 103, 104, 108, 109, 110*
Bloch, F *49*
Bowker, J *30, 114*
Brain, (Lord) W R *106*
Broughton, R *22, 119*
  absurd claim *119*
Byerly, T C & Olsen, M W *104*
Cartlidge *45*
Chalmers *60, 76, 79*
Clarke, C *10, 32, 52, 53, 54, 55, 56, 57, 60, 68, 76*
Clowes, J *74*
Clowes, J & Wassermann G D *101*

Clowes, J & Wassermann, G D *104, 140*
Cook, N D *39*
Cook, S W *92*
Cottingham *54*
Cowan *88*
  theory, weakness of *87*
Cowan, J D *87*
Crick, F *78*
Cupitt, D *78*
Darwin, C *111, 127, 128*
Davenport, C B *103*
Davis, S T *128, 129, 135, 136, 139, 141, 142*
Descartes, R *54, 59, 69, 77, 130*
Dirac, P A M *110*
Doljanski, F *5*
Donnelly, J *142*
Drab, K *84, 85*
Einstein, A *49, 109, 110*
Eysenck, H *108, 111*
Faghoury, M *131*
Fenwick, P *9, 16, 17, 18, 19, 20, 21, 29, 31, 34, 40, 41, 42, 43, 45, 46, 47, 92, 93, 107*

Fermat, P de *142*
Flew, A *131*
Fodor, J A *106*
Fröhlich, H *5, 46, 49, 109*
Gabbard, G O *92*
Geach, P T *131*
Gillett, G R *132*
Glucklich, A *145*
Green, C *37, 63, 72*
Greulich *104*
Grosso, M *31, 33*
Helm, P *131*
Hick, J *137, 139*
Huxley, J *39*
Irish, J A *136, 137*
Irwin, H J *84*
Jacobson, M *56*
Jansen, R I *41, 42, 43, 44*
Jones, F C *92*
Josephson, B D *44*
Jung, C G *118*
Kletti, R *95*
Köhler *68, 78*
Köhler, W *62*
Kolb et al *10, 33, 36, 45, 66, 78, 81, 82, 83, 87, 100, 102, 131, 133, 147*
Lashley, K S *56, 62, 91, 107*
Lazarus, R *24*
Locke, John *75*
Lyon, A *75*
Mackie, J L *132*
Maddox, J *101*
Marks *140*
Meduna, L J *21*
Mekler, L B *39*
Michotte *31*
Moody, R A *16, 17, 21, 25, 26, 83, 89, 91, 93, 94, 96, 97, 98, 99*
Morris *36*

Morse, M *30*
Mott, N *5*
Myers, R H W *24*
Needham, J *103, 104*
Neisser, U *106*
Nevo, E *5*
  world leader in evolutionary studies *6*
Nielsen, K *129, 131, 132, 133, 134, 139*
Noyes, R *95*
Owens, J E *92*
Palay, S L *56, 57*
Penelhum, T *131*
Perry, J *131*
Phillips, D Z *131*
Philo *30*
Planck, M *49, 109*
Popper, K *26, 55*
Popper, K & Eccles, J C *11*
Prabhu, J *139, 140, 144*
Price, H H *142*
Purtill, R L *131*
Putnam, H *57*
Radin, D *26, 36, 118, 119*
Redhead, B *58*
Reichenbach, B *131*
Ring, K *33*
Schrödinger, E *110*
Semon, R *128*
Sheldrake, R *101, 103, 104, 105, 107*
Stevenson, I *11, 29, 75, 92, 143, 145, 146, 147, 148, 149, 150, 151, 153, 155, 156, 157, 158, 159*
Strawson, P *131*
Talbot, M *30, 33*
Teasdale *45*
Twemlow, S W *92*
Vernon, M D *31*
Waddington, C H *128*

170 Gerhard D Wassermann

Wassermann, G 5, 9, 10, 11, 15,
19, 24, 26, 28, 29, 30, 31,
33, 34, 35, 36, 37, 38, 40,
44, 45, 47, 48, 50, 51, 53,
54, 55, 57, 59, 61, 62, 65,
68, 69, 70, 73, 74, 76, 79,
81, 82, 84, 86, 87, 89, 92,
95, 100, 101, 102, 103, 106,
108, 109, 116, 117, 119,
123, 128, 129, 133, 134,
140, 141, 147, 148, 151, 159
associate editor 5
developed a major theory of paranormal phenomena 6
important international conferences 6
speaker 6
visiting professor 5
visiting professor at the Institute of Evolution 5

Wiles, A 142
Williams, B 131
Wood-Jones, F 39

Subject Index

A

Abdallah Abu Hamdan *154, 156*
action-at-a-distance *59*
adaptations *146*
afterlife *17, 36*
  hypothesis *18, 29, 34, 37*
alleles *102, 123, 124*
amino acid molecules *77*
annihilation *137*
anoxia *21, 87*
anti-hallucination hypothesis *41*
anti-materialistic bias *119*
appearance *138*
  the dead *10*
Archimedes' principle *26, 82, 121*
Aristotelian question *74*
association *146*
astronauts *43*
astrophysicists *82*
atoms *81*

B

bad *123*
Beaufort, Sir Francis *99*
beautiful vistas *10*
being of light *16, 94, 97*
Bible *134, 136*
binding problem *78*
biological system *102*
biology *36*
  Theoretical Developmental *6*
Biophilosophy *6*
Birkbeck College *5*
bliss *22*
body *30, 89, 129, 133*
  interior *84*
body and soul *69*
bonds *84*
braille *106*
brain *82, 90, 106, 140, 146*
  alteration in physiology *46*
  disintegrates *15*
  ordinary matter *31, 57, 73*
  physiology *9*
  subjective experience after brain death *47*
bright light *84, 88*
Buddha *144*
buzzing *83, 89*
byproduct *54*

C

Cajal Class I neurons *56*
children *144, 146, 158*
choices *124*
Christianity *129, 136*
clairvoyance *59, 104, 148*
class characteristics *17, 23, 25, 27, 42, 148, 158*
classification *107*
clear sensorium *43*
coevolution *117, 128*
collective unconscious *118*
colour *88*
communication *102, 138*
complete person *135*
complex atoms *72*
complimentarity *68*
concepts *62, 104*
   representing engrams *96*
concert pianists *95*
concommitant development *140*
connectedness *102*
conscious experiences *19, 53, 62, 68, 69*
consciousness *30, 42, 44, 53, 57, 59, 60, 61, 76, 77, 78, 79, 80, 114, 127, 139, 142*
   after death *114*
   as epiphenomena *53*
   entities *79*
   item of *68*
   private *80*
   seat of *73, 114, 135*
consistency argument *34*
contraction *84, 86*
cord *46, 79, 89, 92*
   broken *83*
   elastic *24, 62, 82*
   shimmering *25*
corporeality *141*

creation of important novelty *126*
creationism *139*
creativity *116, 127*
criminals *121*
   super *123*
   'Yorkshire Ripper' *124*
curved space *54*

D

dark matter *82*
dead, the *93, 94, 146*
death *40, 69, 71, 113, 129, 137, 139*
deformability *105*
detached *42*
developmental programs *101*
devil *122*
directed adaptive processes *39*
disembodied *132*
dissolution *129*
DNA *72, 75, 123*
down-quarks *81*
Dreigroschen Oper *135*
dual destination *123*
dualism *60*
dying brain *34, 91*
   hypothesis *29, 34, 35, 37, 40*
      weakness of *38*

E

elastic *83, 84, 147*
   expansion *84*
   system *62*
electromagnetic theory *110*
electron *66*
Elephant Man *137*
embodiment *137*
endorphins *22, 34*
engrams *45, 47, 56, 75, 93, 94, 95, 97, 98, 99, 101, 105, 138, 150*

assesmblies *99*
conscious aspect *56*
two kinds *104*
enigmas *107*
environment *123*
epilepsy *22*
epiphenomena *53, 55, 56, 61, 69*
epiphenomenalism *11, 18, 33, 48, 53, 55*
  alleged refutations of *11*
  modern version *56*
  not a new philosophical insigh *11*
essential part *129*
evil *125, 134, 135*
  born evil *125*
evolution *55, 118, 127, 128*
  adaptive *128*
expansion *147*
explanations *108*
  highly valued *109*

F

faculties *30*
fainting *43*
Falougha *154*
familiarity *159*
feelings *91, 117*
floating *23, 24, 25, 26, 46, 71, 89, 90, 91, 92, 121, 123*
  upwards *23, 25, 42, 82, 83*
forgetting *97*
freewill *79, 124*
Fröhlich oscillators *52*

G

ganzfeld *36*
generic term *53, 54*
genes *70, 71, 75, 115*
  determined by *70*
genetics *121, 123*
genomes *101, 103*

genotype *74*
Gestalt *62, 78*
Gestalt psychologists *27*
Gestalt transformations *62*
Gharife *153*
giant panda *39*
gluons *81*
goal-directed *40*
God *122, 129, 134, 141*
golden light *10*
good *123*
gravitational bonds *82, 83*
Greeks *114*

H

H-SM *82*
  ocean *82*
hallucinations *41, 42, 83, 84, 85, 93*
  multitude of different experiences *41*
hard problem *79*
head to feet *84*
heaven *82, 121, 126, 127, 133, 135, 137, 143*
hell *121, 123, 126, 133, 135, 143*
hereafter *38, 132, 133, 134*
higher dimensional space *52*
Hiroshima *130, 136*
Hitler *117, 122, 124, 126, 134, 141*
Holocaust *134*
human responsibility *124*
hydrogen
  atom *72*
  satom *66*
hypercarbia *20*
hyperskeptics *148*
hypoxia *20*

I

identity *132*

immortality 136
immune system 96
inanimate matter 73
Inquiry 147
inspiration 127
intentionality 78
interact gravitationally 82
internal structure 66
invariance of neuronal circuits 57
inverse square law 59
ions 81

J

joy 22, 93

K

Kaiser, The 135
karma 145
Keller, Helen 137

L

L-SM 82
  body 82
  liberated 82
learned poem 95
life after death 139
life-review 34, 94 95, 95, 96, 97, 98, 99, 100
  predictive theory 110
light 82, 88
  quanta 49
Like influences like 103
localization 55, 72, 101
  parameters 58
looking down on myself 25
love 93

M

macromolecules 81
Mandrake of Oxford 6
material soul 53, 68, 69, 75, 76
material systems 77
materialism 37, 77
mathematics 5, 138
Maung Aye Kyaw 152
meaning
  not in head 57
  representing concepts 57
mechanistic materialism 9, 29, 50, 134, 159
mechanistic materialist 54
mediating systems 90
memory 30, 56, 90, 91, 95, 98, 101, 131, 150, 158
  new 74, 115
  sequence 98
mental
  entities 52
  processes 113
mentality 32, 33, 48, 53, 90, 91, 101, 117, 126, 127, 151
  seat of 42
  secondary encoders 72
  serially ordered 99
messages 127
mind 52, 53, 54, 96
  brain identity 77
  locality of 56
  mind-body problem 47
  non entity 54
  non-localized 10, 32, 46, 47, 51, 56, 57, 68
  not required 54
  useless and redundant 54
miracles 134, 137
models 49, 104
molecules 81
monotheism 51
monozygotic twins 104, 115, 124
moods 117
morphic resonance 101, 102, 103,

104, 106, 107
morphogenesis   *104*
motor equivalence.   *107*
mukhtar   *154*
murderers   *117*
muscles   *107*

N

Nagasaki   *93, 130, 136*
natural selection   *111, 126*
Nature   *83*
NDE   *11, 15, 16, 19, 20, 21, 22, 25, 33, 34, 35, 37, 40, 41, 43, 44, 45, 47, 48, 51, 65, 83, 84, 85, 87, 89, 90, 91, 92, 93, 94, 95, 97, 101, 102, 107, 118, 142*
  anoxia   *19*
  cause of   *20*
  disregarded   *10*
  dying-brain hypothesis   *18*
  explanation   *10, 19, 31*
  nature of   *18*
  near-death experiences   *17*
  new machinery   *10*
necessity   *35*
nervous activity   *107*
nervous system not random   *57*
neural nets   *102, 103*
  criticism   *103*
neurological explanations   *33*
neuronal activity   *42*
neuronal functions   *18*
neurophysiology   *43*
neuroscience   *88*
Newtonian Mechanics   *49*
NMDA receptor   *43*
Nobel Prizes   *49*
normally endowed   *121*

Consciousness & Near Death Experiences 175

O

OBE   *10, 22, 23, 26, 28, 32, 33, 34, 36, 41, 46, 48, 51, 53, 55, 56, 65, 67, 68, 71, 73, 77, 78, 79, 81, 82, 83, 85, 89, 90, 92, 93, 96, 101, 114, 118, 141, 148*
  class characteristics   *83. See also class characteristics*
  disregarded   *10*
  doubles   *28*
  out of the body experiences   *18*
  percipients   *82, 91*
  reality of   *35*
  theory of   *26, 27*
observables   *58*
oil press   *153, 154*
omnipotence   *122*
omniscience   *122*
ordinary matter   *61*
organisms   *73*
outside   *83*
overcrowding   *158*
oxygen loss, speed of   *20*

P

pain   *121, 142*
paranormal   *10, 35, 36, 100*
parapsychology   *36, 45, 59, 102, 115, 118, 119, 148*
  and mechanistic materialism   *159*
  shortcomings   *119*
partially unified explanation   *85*
PCP site   *43*
perceived world   *52*
permanent detachment   *79*
personal identity   *74, 75, 115, 116, 131, 137*
personality   *115, 151*
phantasies   *93*

phenotype *74*
philosophy of science *6, 86*
photo-electric effect *49, 109*
physics *36*
Placido Domingo *116*
planets *118*
playback *17, 95*
pleasure *142*
polypeptide *75*
precognition *148*
predictions *108*
principal invariant *74*
properties *61*
property-detecting systems *62*
proteins *72, 115*
pseudo-exogenous adaptations *39, 128*
psychic phenomena
   spontaneous *36*
psychokinetically *133*
psychology *36, 46*
   normal *48*
psychoneuroimmunology *96*
psychophore *151*
psychophysical isomorphism *68*
purified *123, 134*
purposefullness *39, 117*

Q

qualia *78*
quantum chemistry *73*
quantum electrodynamics *110*
quantum mechanics *5, 6, 59, 72, 110*
quantum view of reality *58*

R

random encounters *152*
random mutations *39*
reality *28, 31, 32*
   argument *35*
   model of *26*

recall *95, 96*
recognition *107*
recollections *99*
reincarnation *10, 11, 29, 50, 116, 143, 144, 148, 150, 153, 158*
   fairy tale *145*
   mechanisms *85, 144, 150*
   personality *146*
   repeated *144*
   Shadow Matter Theory *146*
   subjects *158*
relativity *110*
religion *134, 140*
representation *62*
responsibility *124, 125*
ressurection *129*
resurrection *128, 136*
RNA *72*
   messenger *75*

S

satom *67, 72, 81*
scandal *129*
science
   essential aspects *109*
   new area *76*
seeing *23, 25*
selectron *65, 66, 81*
sensation *92*
separation of bonds *85*
separation process *84*
sequence *99*
Shadow Matter *10, 30, 33, 35, 41, 42, 44, 50, 77, 81, 82, 100, 102, 104, 147*
   body *32, 42, 47, 83, 84, 88, 89, 90, 93, 94, 100, 129, 130, 132, 133, 135, 136*
   brain *19, 27, 31, 42, 43, 44, 45, 47, 48, 51, 53, 54, 55, 56, 58, 59, 60, 61, 62, 67,*

68, 75, 82, 90, 91, 92, 93, 94, 95, 96, 100, 101, 105, 113, 114, 121, 123, 135, 139, 143, 146, 150, 157
  ability to think, feel etc *42*
  detached *149*
  mentality localized in *10*
  OBE *57*
eyes *87, 141*
forces *81*
heavy *82*
light *82*
new science *76*
ocean *117, 121, 123, 127, 133*
selectron *42*
smolecule *42*
soul *130*
theory *89, 95, 119, 147*
thin *84*
turnover *114*
Shadow Matter And Psychic Phenomena *44, 100, 159*
shrink *147*
similarity *103, 104, 105*
simultaneous reactivation *96*
single object *78*
smolecule *66, 67*
smolecules *81*
snapping *83*
snucleus *66*
society *125*
sodium satom *66*
soul *35, 59, 62, 68, 70, 71, 74, 75, 76, 79, 90, 93, 114, 116, 122, 123, 132, 138, 139, 140, 141, 142, 143, 146*
  abnormal *121*
  abnornal *121*
  and Shadow Matter brain identified *59*
  animal *127*
  binding *152*

choices *125*
choices and responsibilities *125*
communication *120*
death *71*
detached could survive indefinitely *59*
energizing system *71*
evil *133*
evolving *118*
genetic aspects *126*
immaterial *59, 60, 75, 142*
immortal *114*
material *30, 59, 60, 61, 113*
migration *133*
model *72*
non-material *69*
normally bonded to the ordinary matter brain *60*
of the listener *70*
piloted *151*
seat of mentality *59*
separate *60*
Shadow Matter brain *30, 117, 126*
survival *70, 118, 120, 122, 138*
spatial properties *61*
special carrier *151*
speculation *121*
sphotons *88*
spirits *16, 137, 138*
spiritualists *11, 69*
splitting *94*
spontaneous phenomena *119*
squark *42, 66, 81*
St Paul *129*
stimulus equivalence *106, 107*
stress *85*
sufficiency *35*
Suleyman *153, 155*
sunlight
  energy from *71*
superconductivity *49, 109*
superstrings *72*

survival 9, 11, 47, 62, 65, 69, 75, 76, 79, 90, 93, 113, 114, 115, 121, 129, 130, 136, 139, 143, 146
  bad punished 12
  communicating souls 116
  good rewarded 12
  highly probable 9
  mechanisms of 15
  offers no final proof 11
  personality 115
  possible mechanisms of 9
  remains a matter of metaphysical belief 11
  Shadow Matter body 38, 69
  soul 116, 118
  two kinds 122
SYMOs 74
system-specific assumptions 49

T

telepathy 51, 59, 70, 102, 104, 116, 118, 120, 122, 132, 138, 142, 151, 152
  theories 120
temporal interval 157
testability 48, 49, 108
  NDEs 50
theory 109
  hypothetico-deductive 48
  natural selection 39
  of everything 50
  of evolution 6
  predictability 49
  using to explain 49
thin layer 84, 87, 88
thoughts 93
three-dimensionality 52
TIMA 39, 40
trance mediums 70, 118
transformation argument 37

transition from TE to OBE 86
triplet of systems 61
tunnel 10, 25, 35, 41, 83, 84, 86, 87, 89, 97

U

ultra heavy 121
unconsciousness 45
University of Newcastle upon Tyne 5, 6
up-quarks 66, 81
upthrust 121

V

validity 108
variations 102
vitalism 147
voice or presence 10

W

wired-in nervous system 56